A Forest in the City
Your Guide to Tryon Creek State Park

A Forest in the City
Your Guide to Tryon Creek State Park

by Friends of Tryon Creek State Park

Designed & Illustrated by Jane Herbst
Edited by Cricket Fegan
Printed by McNaughton & Gunn, Inc., Saline, Michigan

Written in cooperation with Oregon Parks and Recreation Department.

ACKNOWLEDGEMENTS

It has been my great pleasure to observe and work with the dedicated volunteers who have spent two years bringing this book to fruition. Each chapter in the book has been written by a person with specific knowledge in that area, and the reader may find a slight difference of writing style while moving from one chapter to the next, our editor, Cricket Fegan, has worked diligently to ensure the differences are minimal. We have been fortunate to have Jane Herbst as illustrator and book designer, as well as Oregon State Park Naturalist, Michael Niss, as a valuable resource person and writer. I thank our chairperson, Mary May, who led our meetings, and Anita Hamm, Lucille Beck, Daryle Seil and Laura Scott, who worked many hours to research and write the information contained within.

A special thank you goes to Carol Hall, for composing the topographic Tryon Creek State Park map, and METRO's Regional Land Information System for map data. We also extend thanks to Don Barr, retired Geologist, and Glenn Walthall, retired Biologist, who have generously consulted with us, as well as Joe Pesek, Oregon Department of Fish and Wildlife, Larry Campbell, Oregon State University Extension Service, Don Brewer, retired Oregon State University Extension Service Agent, Jim Little, Meteorologist, and Dr. Richard Forbes, Professor of Biology at Portland State University.

It has been through the generous support of the Friends of Tryon Creek State Park's Board of Directors, Oregon Parks and Recreation Department, The Collins Foundation, and the Rose E. Tucker Charitable Trust that we have been able to publish this book. To all, a heartfelt thanks.

We also thank K.C. Craine, Michele Michaud, William Z. Iron, Ruth Pennington, Steve Rice, June Baumler, Sandi Tester, Merle Alexander, Kim Carlson, Fritz Kramer and

Michael Satterwhite for their assistance in putting the book together.

Finally, I would like to express my personal appreciation to all of the volunteers who wrote the copy for the original book on Tryon Creek State Park, *A Guide to An Urban Wilderness*, in the mid-1970's. It is through their example that we have been able to persevere and expand upon the information we offer visitors of the Park today.

Patricia Iron
Executive Director
Friends of Tryon Creek State Park

TABLE OF CONTENTS

INTRODUCTION

Tryon Creek State Park is a 635-acre, natural area located in southwest Portland. The park encompasses a densely forested canyon with a year-round stream, Tryon Creek, flowing through it.

The park is bordered on the west by Boones Ferry Road, on the east by Terwilliger Boulevard, on the north by the Lewis and Clark College Northwestern School of Law, and on the south by the city limits of Lake Oswego. Its location is probably its greatest value, for nearly one half million people – one fifth of the state's population – live within ten miles of the park.

Many visitors are surprised to learn that Tryon Creek is a state park, especially since a substantial part of the acreage lies within the city limits of Portland. Actually four government entities, the City of Portland, Multnomah County, Clackamas County, and the City of Lake Oswego, have jurisdiction over the land near the park's boundaries. The park itself is owned by the State of Oregon and managed by its Parks and Recreation Department. Support services to the park, such as police and fire protection, are provided by the City of Portland.

The mission of the park is to preserve Tryon Creek canyon as a natural area. The park consists of a second-growth forest of Douglas-fir, Western Redcedar, Bigleaf Maple, and Red Alder trees. A wide variety of native shrubs and ground covers provides food and shelter for a large bird population and much small animal life. Tryon Creek and its tributaries widen and deepen the canyon as they flow to the Willamette River.

1

Continued preservation and protection of this undeveloped natural environment, the park's greatest resource, is the primary objective for the use and management of the park. Only those recreational uses compatible with this natural area, such as hiking and running, horseback and bicycle riding, and nature study, are permitted. Development in the park is limited to a 14-mile trail system, Nature Center, covered shelter, parking areas and maintenance facilities. Unlike other state parks, there are no campgrounds, picnic areas, or playgrounds.

"...one time before all time, when there was no season or word, when the stars forgot to dim at dawn, and the meadows held their dew as the sun climbed, then tiny seeds swallowed great vines into themselves and leaped into pods that dwindled older and began. The world began and wind carried its story...the green world grows."

–Kim Stafford

HISTORY

Early History of the Canyon – A Pioneer Family

The source of the name, Tryon, dates back to 1850, with the proving of a donation land claim of 645 acres that included the mouth of the creek and the south part of the canyon. The pioneer was Socrates Hotchkiss Tryon who came to Oregon in 1849.

Socrates Tryon was born in Vermont in 1815. He was well-educated. Soon after receiving a medical degree, he married Frances Safely. In the late 1840's, Socrates traveled to Lahaina in the Sandwich Islands (Hawaii) where he practiced medicine. In one of his letters, still in the hands of his descendants, he wrote: "The King is a fine looking young man about my age. He is very liberal and kind to foreigners...I am to go with the King in his vessel at war."

Tryon left the Islands and came to Oregon in late 1849, subsequently writing to his wife in Iowa that she and infant son, Socrates, Jr., should join him later. His instructions to Frances were for her to come as far as San Francisco by way of the Isthmus of Panama. There she waited with her infant son, operating a boarding house until her husband decided whether to remain in Oregon. The Great Fire of 1851, in San Francisco, settled that. The fire leveled the city, and Frances and three-year-old son came to Oregon to join Socrates. A second child, daughter Sallie, was born later that year.

Tryon's claim was largely forested with virgin Douglas-fir and cedar. He built a small sawmill, farmed an area, and, in 1855, completed a house on the flat area above the Willamette River on what is now known as Stamper Road, just north of the mouth of the creek that was to bear his name. Unfortunately, Tryon's hopes for a good life in Oregon were cut short, for he died, in 1855, at the age of 39. Records indicate the cause of death was sciatic rheumatism.

An interview with his son, S.H. Tryon, Jr., in the Oregon Journal, in 1928, gives a valuable personal recollection of the family's early years here. Socrates, Sr. had left $4,000 to be used for the education of his children, but later events put an end to any hope of prosperity. Frances remarried but was duped by her second husband who absconded with the family's inheritance. As Socrates, Jr. states: "Mother was a Scotch woman and was one of the hardest workers I ever saw. She took a man's place on the farm and in addition did the washing for the girls' school in Oswego." In 1869, Frances Tryon turned over her 645 acres to Socrates, Jr., Sallie, and Sallie's husband, A.A. Cleveland. In 1874, they sold the large tract to the Oregon Iron Company for $7,000, $10.85 per acre.

Early History of the Canyon – Logging & Natural Events

After the Oregon Iron Company purchased the Tryon family land in 1874, logging of the huge cedar and fir began and continued intermittently until the mid-1890's. The timber was used to make charcoal to fire the pig iron foundry in Lake Oswego. The park's present Iron Mountain Trail was established on a major old logging road from this era.

Around 1900, there was a forest fire in the upper canyon. The charred snags, standing for decades, can still be seen today along the northerly section of the Maple Ridge Trail.

Between 1912 and 1915, the canyon again rang with the sound of logging. The Boones Ferry Wood and Tie Company had a logging camp and yard at a site which is

4

now Alfred Street. A sawmill and pond were located in the canyon in the vicinity of the present Beaver Bridge. The lumber, mostly used for railroad ties, fence posts, and cord wood, was hauled out on a "corduroy" road on the east side of the creek and up to a road which is now Fourth Avenue. An old steam donkey engine from this operation was still visible down in the canyon until it was removed when a sewer line was built along the creek in the early 1960's.

Logging resumed again, in the early 1950's, in the south part of the canyon when large cedars and firs were taken out through the Red Fox Meadow, then a dairy farm. The last major logging venture was in 1961, on a 200-acre tract at the north end of the canyon. Fortunately, the firs at the south end of the present Nature Center area were spared, leaving a nice stand along the Big Fir trail.

Two other events, which took a heavy toll on the trees, were the Columbus Day storm, in 1962, and the construction of a major sewer line along Tryon Creek in the early 1960's. The natural growth along the creek was destroyed in this construction, but the regrowth in alder did provide a bountiful harvest for the beaver when they returned.

Effort for a Park – Birth of the Friends

To fully appreciate Tryon Creek State Park, one must understand its unique heritage. Unlike any other state park in Oregon, Tryon Creek was created as the result of a determined community effort to preserve the land. The account leading up to and following the creation of the park is a fascinating story of impassioned citizen involvement that ultimately had a profound effect on the subsequent history of Tryon Creek canyon.

Some provision for a park in the Tryon Creek area reportedly appeared on planning maps as far back as the 1920's, but the idea lay idle for almost 30 years. During the decades of the Great Depression and the Second World War, the ravine was known mainly to local equestrians and venturesome neighborhood children. During that time the Civilian Conservation Corps built an all-purpose trail across the canyon from Dunthorpe to Englewood. The route was used by riders from Oswego Hunt Club and was maintained over the years largely by Englewood resident and horseman, G.H. (Obie) Oberteuffer. Many old-time equestrians have fond memories of fox hunts and paperchases. By modern standards, this suburban area had a slow, sleepy, country atmosphere. Few were concerned with rapid growth and "saving the environment."

However, by the late 1950's, as residential development in the surrounding areas was increasing, interest in the creation of a park was emerging. A committee of the Portland Chamber of Commerce and local government officials held discussions from time to time about a park in the canyon, but money was never available, and the fact that the land lay in two counties and the City of Lake Oswego was a further barrier. No tangible progress was made during that period.

In the early 1960's, the City of Portland built a major trunk sewer alongside Tryon Creek down to Lake Oswego, but, fortunately, local residents defeated a proposal to build connecting sewers in the area. The canyon was therefore still intact, but residential development was on the move and there was increasing recognition by both citizens and government officials that something must be done soon if there was ever to be a substantial park in the canyon.

A breakthrough finally came, in early 1969, when Multnomah County, at the urging of Commissioner David

Eccles, purchased 45 acres on the west side of the canyon bordering Boones Ferry Road. With this first purchase, County officials requested the help of local citizens in promoting a large regional park. Forty enthusiastic supporters rallied to the call at a public meeting held in Lake Oswego in June. From this meeting came a steering committee – G.H. Oberteuffer and Lucille Beck from Englewood, Gary Pagenstecher, Sr., Leonard Kraft, and Jo Simpson from Dunthorpe, Jean Siddall from Lake Oswego, and Brian McDonough from the Boones Ferry area. Their efforts were directed toward establishing a non-profit organization which could promote the project and help coordinate efforts between the local governments.

The organization, Friends of Tryon Creek Park, was incorporated in December, 1969. After securing approval from the City of Lake Oswego for the large park concept, the committee enlisted a number of prominent citizens and agency representatives for the Friends' Board of Directors and Advisors. In addition to the steering committee, other dedicated members included Walter Durham as Treasurer, Barbara Ehman as Secretary, Glenn Gregg, Jack Brown, Marion Talmadge, student Lee Siegel, attorney Paul Gerhardt, Dr. Paul Campbell, Helen Millette, Thyrza Pelling, Janet McLennan, Thornton Munger and George Ruby. Lucille Beck and Jean Siddall served as co-chairpersons.

The first Board meeting of "The Friends", in January, 1970, brought disappointing news that threatened the hope of securing a large park. It was learned that 200 acres in the northern part of the canyon had just been optioned to a developer in Seattle. It was subsequently made known that his plans included the acquisition of additional land and the development of a master plan for the entire canyon, a plan which would have extensive housing development.

With the vision of a large park now in jeopardy, the Friends' Board decided it was essential to take their park plan to the community to gain support. In March, public meetings were held in Lake Oswego, Dunthorpe, and Collinsview, and a fund drive was planned to secure option money for the purchase of additional park lands. The campaign was launched when 325 volunteers set out to canvass their neighborhoods during the first Earth Week in April, 1970. The response to this grass roots effort was overwhelming. During a three week period, 1,400 families, garden clubs, and civic groups contributed $27,000. Nearby schools sponsored events ranging from book sales to sock hops to spaghetti feeds. "Trail Certificates" were a popular memento - each $10 bought one foot of trail in the park. The success of this campaign spurred contagious enthusiasm that swept the community and broadened public support for the park.

During the summer of 1970, the Friends took contracts on two parcels of land, 28 acres on the Terwilliger side and 13 acres on Boones Ferry Road. But, despite these successes, the problems were enormous, both financial and political. It was determined that the 200 acres planned for development were important for the park, since they provided the largest flat areas in the canyon. Unfortunately, efforts to negotiate a contract on this land were unsuccessful. By October, the plan for development on the 200 acres was progressing, and a hearing was scheduled for November.

Time was running out and it was imperative to find additional funding sources, both public and private. The large regional park was to be about 600 acres and the cost was estimated at around two million dollars. Friends of Tryon Creek offered to raise 25% of the funds if the local governments would contribute 25% and obtain Federal matching funds. While the Friends' commitment was

8

undoubtedly possible with considerable effort, the local governments were noncommittal. Where was all the money to come from?

In early October, the Friends' co-chairs Beck and Siddall met with Glenn Jackson, chairperson of the State Highway Commission and holder of the purse strings for Oregon State Parks. The State did not create parks in cities, but it was hoped they might provide some financial assistance. Jackson was a man of few words and great vision. Recognizing both the political and financial problems for a regional park, he quickly responded: "We can't share in this. It would open up a can of worms all over the State. I think the whole thing probably should be a State Park." The basis for his decision was threefold - the canyon was a large area still intact, it was where people lived, and, perhaps most important, the Tryon project had enormous community support. With that decision, he had reversed previous state park policy.

In the following week, Federal matching funds were secured, and Tryon Creek State Park was announced, with suitable fanfare, by Governor Tom McCall. Oregon was to have its first urban state park! Headlines blazed with the good news and park supporters everywhere were euphoric.

However, the establishment of the park was not to be a simple matter. The hearing for the 200-acre development plan was still scheduled before the Multnomah County Planning Commission in November and political problems continued. In September, the Commission had approved the boundaries for the park all the way up to Terwilliger if money could be found, but since the State had not yet been able to purchase this 200 acres, the Planning Commission gave preliminary approval to the development plan. In effect, they approved the development on the same land they had already approved for a park. Another hearing was set for December. The future of the park was still uncertain. Park enthusiasts and donors were dismayed at this turn of events, but the Friends and the community backers were undaunted. The December hearing overflowed with hundreds of park supporters. The Planning Commission had received over 90 letters, including one from Governor McCall, strongly endorsing the whole park. The voice of the people had indeed been heard. The development plan was withdrawn, and the hearing ended in triumphant jubilation.

With the complete park now assured, the State could go ahead with acquisition. In January, 1971, at the first anniversary meeting of Friends of Tryon Creek, Glenn Jackson presented the deed for the 200-acre tract acquisition which had been a major obstacle. Tryon Creek State Park was officially born.

During 1971-72, the State purchased the remaining available properties in the canyon, bringing the total park to 620 acres. At that point, the park, at a total cost of over 3 million dollars, was fully established.

Master Plan and Nature Center

In order to ensure that Tryon Creek would remain a natural park, the State undertook development of a detailed master plan to identify all the natural resources and determine appropriate uses of the park. This was a process not previously used in other state parks. In the master plan the location of trails for hikers and equestrians, a perimeter bicycle trail and a nature center area were determined. The only buildings permitted were to be for interpretation of the natural environment. One of the park's greatest assets was its urban location, and the need to protect its natural values was recognized.

The Friends of Tryon Creek and the State were in agreement that a nature interpretive building would be not only an appropriate focal point, but would also be an asset in promoting good use of the park for both recreation and education. It was envisioned that such a facility would enhance visitors' appreciation and understanding of the natural world and would encourage a sense of stewardship for the land. While recreational use would follow naturally, the opportunity for educational use needed to be fostered through an interpretive center.

Since State funds for such a project were very limited, Friends of Tryon Creek made the decision to plan and build a nature center building and shelter as a gift to the Park from the community. A major fund drive was necessary and was begun with a memorable kick-off event, "Trail Days," on a weekend in April, 1973. Board member Jean Siddall flagged trails and recruited 'bosses' to supervise this major trail-building effort. Some 300 people turned out to take hazel hoes, shovels, loppers, and chain saws in hand. Several miles of trail were cleared and graded, including the nature center loops in use today. It was a beautiful weekend and an enormous accomplishment by the community.

The Friends engaged Curtis Finch, of Lake Oswego, as the architect, and planning got underway. Although there were many nature centers in the mid-West and East, this concept was new to the Northwest, and there was no model. Much brainstorming went on, and a visit to centers in Michigan and Minnesota affirmed the Friends' objectives and plans.

With several foundation grants and many contributions from the community at large, the Friends raised $130,000 for the nature center and shelter. The State added $50,000 to complete the fund and also provided the access road, parking area and all utilities. Construction was begun in

1974, and was completed in the spring of 1975. The general contractor was R.A. Gray & Co., and Glenn Gregg, from the Friends' Board, acted as clerk-of-the-works, overseeing the project to its completion.

The nature center facility was an enormous undertaking for a citizen group, but it turned out exceedingly well, and the cooperative relationship between the State and Friends of Tryon Creek was firmly established. Throughout this whole process of planning and building, the Friends received continuing support from State Parks Director Dave Talbot. Though it was a new experience for the State to work with a citizen group, the value of such a partnership was recognized and set the stage for similar arrangements to be developed in other state parks.

The unique history of Tryon Creek State Park represents several "firsts" in the Oregon State Park System. It was the first in a city, the first to have a master plan, the first to have a citizen group involved, the first to have a nature center, and the first to have an "all-abilities" trail for visitors.

Tryon Creek State Park was officially dedicated in July, 1975, when Highway Commission Chairperson Glenn Jackson addressed a crowd of dignitaries and community residents.

A Unique Partnership – The Friends and the State

The opening of the nature center, in 1975, set the stage for the continuing partnership between Friends of Tryon Creek and the Oregon Parks and Recreation Department. Visitors are often unaware of how broadly the Friends' volunteer organization is involved in support of this park's operation.

Essentially, the State owns, manages, and maintains the park and facilities. Even though the Friends were largely responsible for construction of the building and nearby shelter, the group does not retain ownership. The State provides a Park Manager and support personnel, including a Naturalist, who is the key person at the nature center. The Naturalist, whose responsibilities involve interpretation and public liaison, works closely with the Friends on projects and activities. Ongoing maintenance of the trails is accomplished by Park Rangers, often working with outside groups or volunteers. Maintenance of the building also receives their high priority.

Efforts of the Friends of Tryon Creek have been directed largely toward educational programs, volunteer services, and special events or projects. Over the years the Friends' activities have increased manyfold, requiring a full-time Executive Director who supervises volunteers and ongoing activities and works closely with the Board of Directors. This individual has secured foundation grants for several special projects. An Education Director manages a busy program for schools, as well as offerings for the public such as the Sunday-at-Two lecture series. Volunteers serve as school guides, receptionists, and, in a myriad of helpful ways, in park activities. A Nature Day Camp Director is engaged to run the very successful summer program.

The Friends' Board is actively involved in implementing ongoing programs, special events, and projects. Established activities include the Nature Day Camp, Summer Forest Music Concerts, a gift store, and annual events – the Trillium Festival, Tryonathon, and a holly and wreath sale. Membership, publications, fund-raising, and land acquisition are all areas of Board participation. The Friends also sponsor a photo club and a Daytripper hiking group. Permanent major projects, the all-abilities Trillium Trail, contour relief map in the nature center, and outdoor information kiosk were undertaken by the Friends with assistance from the State.

Certainly the time, talents, and energy of people from the community have been an enormous asset to the park. With the excellent management and continuing support from State Parks staff, the partnership here has been an outstanding example of government and citizens working together. It has given an extra dimension to Tryon Creek which could not be achieved by either entity alone. Indeed, the success of this first unique partnership has prompted the State to promote similar volunteer groups in a number of other parks.

"In Wilderness is the preservation of the earth."

–Thoreau, *Walden*

14

GEOLOGY

Tryon Creek State Park lies in the northern part of the Willamette Valley, south of Portland and just north of the city of Lake Oswego. Many millions of years and a multitude of geologic events have created the landscape of the park and its adjacent land. There are a number of these events that have given shape to the present Willamette Valley and the Portland basin, including Tryon Creek State Park. These geologic processes included volcanoes, faulting, folding, earthquakes, and catastrophic flooding. The geology of the park is just a small part of the overall picture of the area.

Approximately 40 million years ago, a land mass of volcanic origin lay off the Oregon coast. At that time, the ancient sea shore lay very close to the east part of what is now the Portland basin. The land lay submerged until about 28 million years ago when it was elevated above the water. It was a relatively flat terrain, and it consisted of volcanic flows and associated sediments containing fossil sea creatures. Subsequently it was much eroded.

The theory of plate tectonics assumes that the lithosphere is broken into individual plates that move in response to convection currents in the upper mantle. Illustrating this theory, is the Waverly Heights Formation, as exposed in Tryon Creek State Park. It is considered to be part of an island that was rafted on an oceanic plate millions of years ago. The formation is exposed in most of the park proper and some areas surrounding the park, including Waverly Heights on the east side of the Willamette River. It was in place before the subsequent period of major volcanic activity, that of the outpouring of the Columbia River basalts. About 15 million years ago, the Columbia River basalts began to spill out of huge cracks in the earth near the Idaho, Washington, and Oregon borders. These basaltic flows spilled over much of southwest Washington and continued flowing into the northern part of Oregon. Some of the early flows followed the early course of the Columbia River, which dumped into the ocean near Salem, Oregon. Successive flows of the basalts filled in some of the channels of the Columbia River, moving it farther and farther north to its present location. The basalts flowed around the Waverly Heights basalt but did not flow over the top. This is why the Park is composed mostly of Waverly Heights basalts.

There were many other Columbia River basalt flows. Between some of the flows, there were spans of thousands of years for erosion to take place, forests to grow, lakes to form, before the next basalt flows covered them up. Evidence for this is in the petrified wood, tree casts, and other plant material found between some of these layers of basalt.

Close to the south end of Tryon Creek State Park where Terwilliger and State streets meet, there is a tree cast at the base of the cliff. A number of such tree casts can also be seen about 1,000 feet east on the north side of Highway 205 at the West Linn wayside.

There were 14 flows of Columbia River basalts in the Portland basin. The basalts are about 1,000 feet in thickness. The most common rock in the Lake Oswego area is Columbia River basalt with the exception of the Waverly Heights basalts of the park. These Columbia River basalts are assigned to the Miocene Epoch.

The Pacific Plate's diving under the North American Plate caused the Coast range to arch up with the Portland Hills. This caused down-folding of the Portland-Vancouver-Tualatin Basins including the land which is now Lake Oswego. The east side of the upfold was dropped, due to the Portland

Hills fault, during this period. As the Portland Basin was dropped lower and lower by the action of the fault, a large lake formed, and the Columbia River dumped first mudstone and later gravels into it, creating a depth of 1,725 feet. A later period of deposition, the Troutdale Gravels, was dumped into this basin up to an elevation of 625 feet.

The Troutdale Gravels contained a percentage of rocks called quartzites. The quartzites are metamorphosed quartz sand, like white beach sand. In some places the quartzites make up 30% of the gravels.

Exposures of these gravels can be seen on the sides of the Mt. Tabor cinder cone, on Cornell Road just before the road enters the first tunnel, and good exposures can be seen along the lower Sandy River several miles south of Troutdale. The late Dr. James Stauffer, Professor of Geology and Biology at Lewis and Clark College, indicated seeing Troutdale Gravels in a lower stretch of Tryon Creek in the park.

A number of other faults developed during this period. The Lake Oswego fault goes through the lake of the same name. The Iron Mountain fault parallels the Iron Mountain Road close to the Hunt Club where a number of homes are built on the edge of that fault scarp. The faulting there also caused the south side of Lake Oswego to be dropped several hundred feet. The Oatfield-Terwilliger fault follows along Terwilliger Boulevard on the east side of the park. Another small fault cuts across the southern end of the park.

Some 2 million years ago, more volcanic activity took place, and these volcanoes are called the Boring Lavas. There were many of these small volcanoes dotting the skyline between the Portland area and the town of Boring, Oregon. Two, in the vicinity of the Park, are Mount Sylvania and Cook's

Butte. These two volcanoes are similar to Mount Tabor and Mount Scott on the east side of the city. Both produced lava flows and some ash. A Mount Sylvania flow entered the western edge of the park and lies on the Waverly Heights formation and the Columbia River basalts.

The Boring Lavas were named by a geologist, Ray Treaher, for a cluster of vents close to the town of Boring, a few miles east of Portland. There are many of these vents close to the Portland-Lake Oswego area, including Rocky Butte, Mount Scott, Kelly Butte, Highland Butte, and Mount Sylvania, to name a few. Cook's Butte, which is closest to Lake Oswego, dates back 1.3 million years.

Tryon Creek State Park is unique in that this small area of the park and land, extending under Lewis and Clark College and down to the Willamette River, is a different kind of rock, 26 million years older than the rest of the rock in this area.

The most exciting geologic period, for the park and Willamette Valley, was the Ice Age, beginning some 3 million years ago and ending around 12,000 to 10,000 years ago. Within this 3 million years of time, the continental glaciers covered about 55% of North America.

There were mountain glaciers in the Cascades. The continental and mountain glaciers went through times of retreating and expanding. For example, about 12,000 years ago, a lobe of the continental glacier plugged the Clark Fork River in Montana, forming a huge lake called Lake Missoula. Successively, the lake would fill with many cubic miles of water before the plug released.

Similarly, The Bretz Floods, so named because they were described by geologist J. Harlen Bretz, occurred during the last 2,000 years of the Ice Age. A tongue of the ice sheet plugged the Clark Fork River and released the water about every 55 years. It has been estimated that there were at least 40 floods and possibly as many as 100. During these time spans, when the dam broke, the water would rush over southeast Washington, down the Columbia River through the Wallula Gap toward the Portland area, and up the Willamette River to Eugene. At times it ran into barriers such as ice jams that would cause the water to pond into large lakes.

One such lake was Lake Allison in the Willamette Valley. The water in the Portland-Lake Oswego-Tryon Creek area was about 400 feet above sea level. This meant that Lake Oswego was under about 200 feet of water and the park area was under about 100 to 150 feet of water. The rushing water also scoured the land down to the basalts of the Waverly Heights Formation.

In other places, as the force of the water slowed down, it would drop its load of debris to form blockages or debris dams. An example of this type of blockage is the debris that blocked the Tualatin River and changed its course so that it entered the Willamette River, some 6 miles farther south of its original course.

Before the Bretz Floods, the Tualatin River flowed through what is now Lake Oswego. As the water rushed through this area, it widened the valley and created the Lake Oswego lake bed.

Between the great floods, there were long dry periods. The fine sediments deposited in the Portland basin were then blown around by these dry winds. This left deposits of fine silts on the surrounding lands, but, with each successive flood, the loose sediments on the hill were washed away.

Remnants of these sediments are still on surrounding hills above where the flood waters flowed.

Since the Ice Age, Tryon Creek has helped cut down through the Waverly Heights volcanics to provide many habitats for plants and animals. The relationship between the park's geological resources and its various inhabitants is still dynamic and everchanging.

"We are as much alive as we keep the earth alive."

–Chief Dan George

SOIL

Soil is composed of layers of stone, sand, and clay which has been worn away by the elements and living things, a collection of natural bodies which has been synthesized in profile form from a mixture of broken and weathered minerals and decaying organic matter. This mantle of soil covers the earth in a thin layer, which supplies support and sustenance for plants. Soil is made by the action of water, wind, glacial action, and acids produced by pioneer plants such a liverworts, mosses, and lichens.

How a soil feels to the touch is one way of determining soil type. Clay soils feel very slick and tend to make a ribbon when pressed or rolled between the fingers. Silt has a floury or talcum powder feel when dry and is only slightly sticky when wet. Sand particles feel gritty to the touch.

The soil in Tryon Creek State Park has a very hard clay layer, fragipan, 24 inches under the surface. Most tree roots and water cannot penetrate this hard clay layer. During the winter this makes the ground very wet and unstable. When a strong wind or ice storm strikes the park after a rainy period, many trees lose their grip in the wet, shallow soil and fall over.

The upper soil layer in the park is rich in humus. This dark colored mulch contains the decaying remains of roots, leaves, and other plant materials. Many animals live in this soil layer, and their activities such as eating, tunneling, and excreting enhance the decay process which in turn speeds the flow of nutrients to the roots of living plants. Thus, the forest recycles its nutrients through its blanket of soil.

CLIMATE

Climate is the sum of all the weather elements affecting a particular location: wind, temperature, and the amount and distribution of precipitation. The microclimate of an area includes all of these along with the additional influences of vegetation, orientation, and slope. Tryon Creek's overall climate is similar to the rest of the Portland area. However, its unique location, dense forest canopy, and water sources contribute to a distinct microclimate that dictates the types of plants and animals that thrive in the park.

The temperatures at the park are quite mild. The average summer-winter temperature range is a July maximum of 80F and a January minimum temperature of 33F. Visitors enjoy escaping the summer heat while taking a walk in the shade of the forest or enjoying a picnic in the shelter.

The average growing season is a little over 200 days with dry, moderately warm summers and wet, mild winters. Measurable precipitation falls about 160 days a year, the result of frequent storms that move in from the Pacific Ocean in the winter, and occasional showers and even a stray thunderstorm in the summer.

The Tryon Creek watershed receives an average of about 40 to 45 inches of moisture a year, with 70% falling from November through March and an average 5% from June through August. In some years, no precipitation falls during periods of 30 to 60 days during the summer. The effect of these substantial seasonal variations on creek fluctuation can be observed as one walks along the trail and crosses the bridges.

Despite the protection from the Coast Range, Pacific storms can occasionally generate winds of considerable strength at

Tryon Creek State Park. This occurs from October to April with winds of sustained speeds of 40 to 50 miles per hour during most years. During the Columbus Day storm of 1962, winds in excess of 70 mph ranged throughout the Willamette Basin. Trees which have been toppled are a regular sight in the park.

Marine air often covers the Willamette Valley bringing morning clouds or fog. The summertime high sun-angle brings sufficient solar energy to evaporate the clouds for pleasant, sunny afternoons. The east winds in this area exert a strong influence on park temperatures. They can bring bitterly cold air to this area in the winter and hot, dry air in the summer. During an east wind condition in the summer, for example, the humidity may drop as low as 15% to 20% with a resultant high fire hazard.

Diamonds

Cups of fresh wood sorrel hold
rain jewels in their dimples.
We beggars forget our needs
and appraise the transient hoard
with pleasure. Ah, rain–

–Anita Hamm

WHERE THE RIVER RUNS - THE CREEK ENVIRONMENT

Where does Tryon Creek begin? Where does it end? And what happens to it between these two points? The first two questions are relatively easy to answer. However, even an expert would have trouble answering the third.

Where does the creek begin? Tryon Creek is a short, perennially flowing stream that drains a small watershed north of Lake Oswego, south of the Capitol Hill area, and east of the West Portland Hills.

The creek originates as a series of seeps and springs in the hills near the park. These trickles merge to form small seasonal and year-round tributaries. Tryon Creek first appears as a blue line, on most maps, near Marshall Park in Southwest Portland. From there, the creek flows southeast through private property until it enters the park just north of Boones Ferry Road. Near this point, the flow from a major tributary, Arnold Creek, joins Tryon Creek to form the main stream through the park.

Tryon Creek is only 7 miles long and is characterized by a large seasonal fluctuation in water levels. In the winter, between November and February, the stream carries a large volume of run-off that cannot infiltrate the soaked, low permeability soils and the paved and built-on areas surrounding the park. The water rages down the creek bottom and spreads over its narrow flood plain, carrying large quantities of light, silty soil. The channel is modified in places, as logs, gravel, and brush pile up in jams and divert the stream flow.

Through the spring and fall, the water level drops and changes from a muddy brown color to a fairly clear

24

appearance. Some of its volume is still composed of runoff, but most of the water is now flowing out of underground aquifers through springs and seeps.

All through the dry summer, Tryon Creek and its primary tributaries continue to flow. The creek has cut a canyon into an important aquifer, the Troutdale Formation. Clear water surfaces through the streambed, and, in many places, flows through the soils composing the narrow floodplain. The wet spots, visible along the trails even after weeks of dry weather, are evidence of this near-surface water flow.

Tryon Creek is actively cutting its channel and canyon deeper. The stream profile shows a fairly steep gradient, especially toward the south end of the park where basalt bedrock is at the surface. The riffles and small pools, created by the exposed rock, give the creek a "mountain stream" appearance in this area, as opposed to its sluggish, meandering nature visible from most of the bridges.

Where does Tryon Creek end? The Willamette River is the final destination for Tryon Creek. Large pipes under State Street (Highway 43) carry the water back on to private property. From here, the creek flows past the Tryon Creek Wastewater Treatment Plant into the Willamette. The creek has flowed less than 10 miles from its origins to its destination.

What can one discover along the creek? Five footbridges cross Tryon Creek. An enjoyable way to experience the environment along the creek is to walk the section of Middle Creek Trail between High Bridge and Beaver Bridge.

At High Bridge, Tryon Creek takes on its typical appearance through the park: a sluggish, meandering stream with dense forest vegetation growing to the water's edge. The muddy banks are steep in places and quite slippery.

As one starts walking toward Beaver Bridge, one is in the creek's narrow floodplain. However, this area rarely floods and, as a result, forest trees and shrubs are reclaiming this flat location. Red Alder trees, with their mottled grayish white bark, are in abundance. The common spiny shrub growing along the trail here is Salmonberry.

The next major feature one encounters on this walk is a board walk that spans a boggy section of trail. The water table is at or near the surface here, and the soil stays damp year around. Plants associated with wet soils grow here. Skunk Cabbage, with its huge green leaves and pungent yellow flowers in early Spring is a good indicator of soggy soils.

Beyond the board walk, Middle Creek Trail veers away from the creek. Typical forest trees such as Western Redcedar and Western Hemlock grow along the trail.

As one approaches Beaver Bridge, the tangle of vegetation that lines the creek becomes evident. Shrubs, such as Red Elderberry and Salmonberry, thrive in the sunlight and damp soils. This dense growth makes walking along the water very difficult.

A variety of animals lives along and within the creek. Aquatic insects and crayfish hide under rocks and submerged tree limbs. Frogs and salamanders hunt for food in the dense undergrowth next to the water. Great Blue Herons and raccoons search for crayfish and tadpoles in the sluggish water. Beaver cut down streamside alders for food.

During its brief passage, Tryon Creek has shaped the land, watered shoreline plants, and provided water, food and shelter for many animals. And finally, the creek has given this popular state park a beautiful focal point!

"Some consider blue to be the color of pure water, whether liquid or solid. But looking down into our waters...they are seen to be of different colors...blue at one time and green at another, even from the same point of view."

–Thoreau, *Walden*

THE CHANGING FOREST

Tryon Creek State Park is one of the largest forested parks in the Portland area. As one walks or rides through the park, one might think that this dense stand of surrounding trees is the original forest. But this woodland is very different from the one that grew here when the first settlers arrived in the 1850's. And the forest that will grow here in the year 2,050 will be different from the one visited today.

As the first Oregon Trail settlers entered the north end of the Willamette Valley, they were in awe of the forests they saw. Huge Douglas-firs and Western Redcedars towered above them. Scattered among the ferns and maples on the forest floor were moss covered logs that were toppled by windstorms many years before. These long-dead trees were larger than any living trees growing "back East". Undoubtedly, these practical pioneers saw the beauty of the original forest, but necessity forced them to make a living off this new land.

The land that is now the park was logged between 1880 and 1920. Most of the large Douglas-firs and Western Redcedars became charcoal and lumber.

Logging changed the forest dramatically. The cool, shady woods became open fields exposed to the sun. Grasses, shrubs, and wildflowers flourished.

Soon, however, the trees started to return. Red Alder, Bigleaf Maple, and Douglas-fir seedlings thrived in these areas disturbed by logging and forest fires. They are now the oldest and tallest trees in the park.

As the firs, maples, and alders grew and shaded the forest floor, conditions were right for more shade-tolerant trees

28

such as Western Hemlock and cedar. The conditions that favor certain plants might not favor others. Also, the conditions created by certain plants might not favor their offspring. For example, the shade created by the large Douglas-fir trees actually inhibits fir seedlings from growing underneath their parents. This progression of plant change, called succession, is at work in the forest one walks and rides through the park today.

And the forest at Tryon Creek will continue to change. The alders and maples will eventually be replaced by the Western Redcedars and hemlocks. The Douglas-firs will continue to grow above the other trees. The understory plants will also change with the trees as the forest matures. In another century or two, the forest may begin to resemble the one that the early settlers marvelled at. Or, the successional clock might move a step backward if a disturbance such as a fire or windstorm opens the forest floor to sunlight and bare soil again.

Natives and Non-Natives

Besides the natural process of succession, the forest at Tryon Creek State Park has changed in other ways. Several plants growing in the park today do not belong here! These non-natives have been introduced over the years and now have a firm foothold in the forest. Some, like daffodils and apple trees, are not widespread. Others, such as English Ivy and Garlic Mustard, are widespread and are taking over sections of the forest floor.

How did these non-native plants find their way into the park? Some were planted here before the park was created. Many have escaped from neighborhood gardens. Their seeds have been carried into the park on the wind, on the fur of mammals, and in the droppings of birds.

Do the non-native plants harm the forest? In most cases the native plants can successfully compete with the non-natives for sunlight, water, and growing space. However, certain aggressive species can overwhelm the natives and take over. English Ivy *(Hedera helix)* is the best example. Native to Europe and the Mediterranean region, this shade-loving plant was brought to Oregon gardens and has escaped into the forest. This evergreen vine grows by trailing stems that take root as they creep along the forest floor. Seeking sunlight, the vine will eventually climb tree trunks and reach the canopy. There it will flower and produce berries that are eaten by birds. The seeds are then spread further into the forest in bird droppings.

Ivy such as this can damage native plants in several ways. It can completely cover the forest floor, depriving other plants of sunlight, water, and growing space. Once it gets into the canopy, the aggressive vines can wrap around the tree's growing tip, depriving it of sunlight and weakening it. The weight of hundreds of pounds of living ivy plants on a weakened tree may result in the tree blowing down during a windstorm. Consequently, park staff and volunteers are involved in an ongoing effort to remove English Ivy from the park.

"Remember what you have seen because everything forgotten returns to the circling winds."

– Navajo Wind Chant

PLANTS

"The array of life the nurse log suckles is but one visible episode of intensity in the whole busy weave of the grove. Both virgin and nurse, the hospitality of an old tree is like the crushing embrace of a grandmother starved by absence from her young kin, but the embrace continues for centuries...I read a tree's gesture, an old one's silence."

–Kim Stafford

DISCLAIMER

Plant ethno-use is included for informational purposes only. It is not meant to be a definitive listing of edible plants. As with all wild edibles, we advise you to seek more authoritative sources. We do not recommend your picking or eating any of these plants, since these practices are not allowed in an Oregon state park.

31

GROUND COVERS AND WILDFLOWERS

Alum Root *(Heuchera micrantha)*
Grows to 3 feet. Leaves, basal, round or heart-shaped with 5 to 11 lobes, length about 2 to 3-1/2 inches. Some leaves turn red before they die, but most last all winter long. Small white flowers grow on side branches from a tall stalk. Lives in moist crevices or outcroppings of rock.

Native peoples pounded the plant and placed it on the hair of little girls to make it grow thick. The plant was also used on cuts.

Bleeding Heart *(Dicentra formosa)*
Erect-stemmed plant grows 8 to 18 inches tall. From a creeping rhizome, leaves and stems grow upright. Leaves with bluish tinge grow on stalks 9 to 20 inches long. Each leaf has long, compound, fern-like leaflets. Flowers, which appear March to July, are small, pink or lavender, heart-shaped, growing in clusters. Fruit is plump pod about 1/2 to 2 inches long. Found in damp shady spots, open woods in moister climate.

Skagit tribe used it as worm medicine, as cure for toothache, and hair wash.

Candy Flower or **Siberian Miner's Lettuce** *(Montia sibirica)*
Long-petioled basal leaves. Flowers pink or white, with candy cane stripes on petals. Hence, the name "candy flower". Some plants are annual, others perennial with rhizomes. Grows in sun or shade.

Edible green lettuce for miners, as well as natives, in the gold rush of 1849.

Candy Flower

Cleavers Bedstraw *(Galium aparine)*
Annual with weak, climbing or trailing stems 1 to 3 inches long. Square, hairy, and rough stems. Six to 8 leaves in a whorl, 1/2 to 1-1/2 inches long. Four petaled, white flowers, less than 1/4 inch across, grow in clusters at end of branches. Fruit has short hooked hairs. Common plant that grows in shady places.

Cowlitz women rubbed their bodies with it while bathing to become lucky in love. It was a love charm for Quileute women, and used as bedding also.

Dandelion *(Taraxacum officinale)*
Grows 3 to 30 inches tall. Leaves and flower stalks clustered at base of plant. Yellow flowers grow on hollow stalks. Seed about 1/8 inches long and brownish-gray tipped with stalk 2 to 4 times as long, which is topped with feathery, white bristle end. It is found everywhere.

Leaves sometimes used as food for silkworms. Humans have used it since ancient times. Greens are eaten in spring before flower appears. Good source of Vitamin A, calcium, and potassium. Flowers used in making wine and native people used stems as chewing gum. Europeans used it to treat jaundice and gallstones. Chinese used it to treat colds, bronchitis, pneumonia, boils, and ulcers.

Duckfoot or **Inside-out Flower** *(Vancouveria hexandra)*
Grows 6 to 20 inches tall. Leathery leaves are divided 1 to 3 times into 3's, almost as wide as long (1-1/2 inches), which gives plant its common name. Small, pointed, white flowers appear May to July. Blooms have 6 longer sepals which are bent back giving the stamens an elongated look, hence its other common name. Usually found in shady, coniferous forests.

34

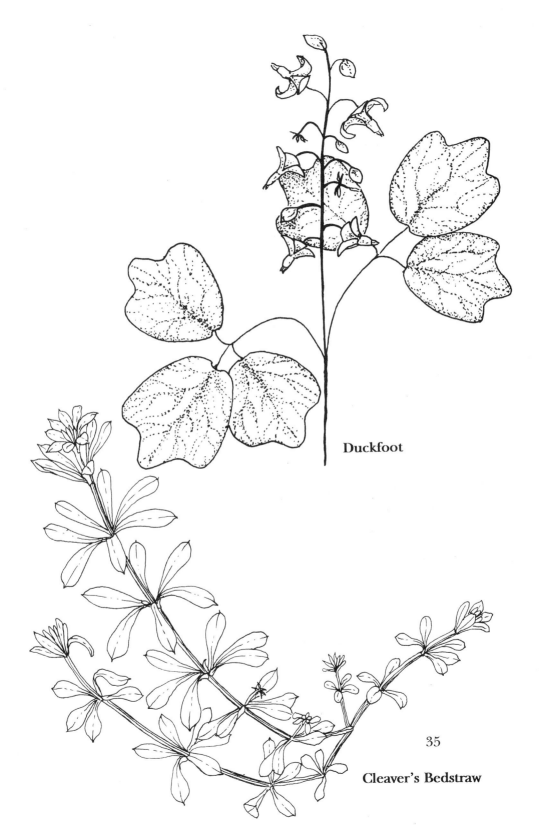

Duckfoot

35

Cleaver's Bedstraw

Fairy Bells *(Disporum hookeri)*
Grows 1 to 3 inches tall with downy or somewhat hairy stems.
Bright green leaves, also somewhat downy, are 2 to 3 inches
across, tightly clasp stem. Creamy, bell-shaped flowers hang
in groups of 2 to 5 from branch tips. Stamens are longer
than petals and sepals. Berries ripen in late summer, are
ovoid and range from bright orange to scarlet. Fairy Bells
are often found with Fairy Lanterns in moist, shady woods.

Used by the Makah as a love potion. Most tribes considered
the plant highly poisonous and had little use for it.

False Hellebore *(Veratrum californicum)*
Broad, strongly-ribbed lengthwise leaves, 3-1/2 to 4 feet tall
plant. Leaves are stalkless and heavily veined, grow 8 to 10
inches long and point upwards. Small, 3/4 to 1 inch, white
flowers grow in dense clusters on erect stalks, have 3 petals
and 3 sepals, sometimes greenish near base, appear June to
August. Extremely poisonous. Pregnant sheep that have
eaten it give birth to lambs with deformed heads, and
flowers are poisonous to insects. Grows in marshy areas and
moist forests.

Quinault boiled it for tea to treat rheumatism. Cowlitz tied
a leaf around arm to relieve pain.

False Lily-of-the-Valley or **May Flower** *(Meianthemum dilatatum)*
Heart-shaped leaves clasp 4 to 10 inch stem. Excellent
ground cover with sweet perfume. White flower has 2 petals,
2 sepals and 4 stamens. Fruit shiny, speckled brown turning
to dull red. Found in shady, moist woods.

Natives used the plant to apply to sore eyes.

36

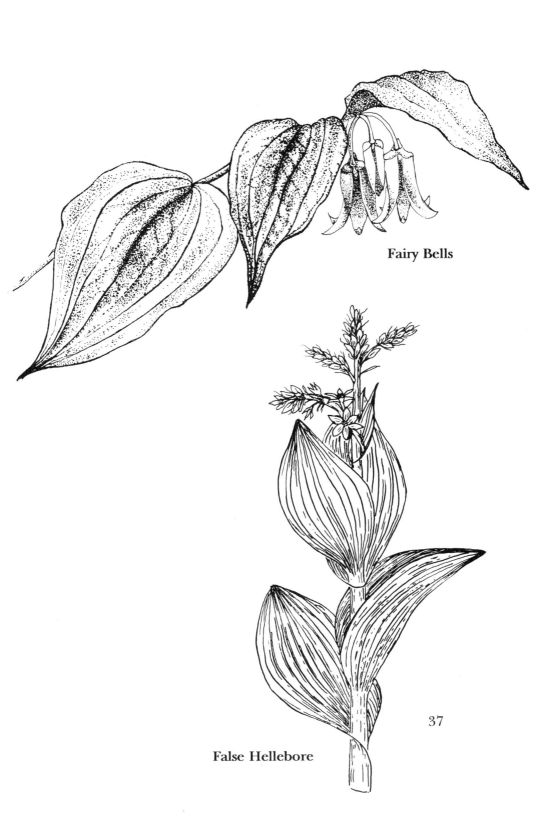

Fairy Bells

37

False Hellebore

False Solomon's Seal *(Smilicina racemosa)*
Commonly leaning plant grows to 3 feet tall. Narrow, oval, shiny leaves about 3 to 8 inches long clasp stem at base. Dense clusters of tiny, white, 1/10 inch-long flowers in plumes appear on end of branches in March to July, with 6 oval petal-like segments and 6 stamens that are slightly longer. Fruit is mottled green and red berry, about 1/4 inch long, that turns deep red when ripe. Found in moist woods.

Paiute and Shoshone used plant as a contraceptive, a cathartic, a cure for sore throat and lung disease. Berries eaten by ruffed grouse and have been eaten by humans to avoid scurvy; too many may have a laxative effect.

Fireweed *(Epilobium augustifolium)*
Perennial plant with no branches on an erect stem that grows 3 to 8 feet tall. Four to 6-inch narrow leaves with looped veins at edge. Rose-purple flower stalks bloom June to September with 4 petals and 4 sepals, 1/2 to 3/4 inch long. Long, thin, 2 to 3-inch pod grows out rigidly from stem. Tender shoots are cooked as greens and dry, mature leaves can be used for tea. Grows densely in logged or burned over areas.

Puget Sound Indians used shoots as a laxative, a root decoction for sore throat, as a tonic and astringent.

Fragrant Bedstraw *(Galium triflorum)*
Perennial with weak stems either erect or trailing, 8 to 18 inches long from creeper rootstock. Leaves in whorl of 6. White flowers in clusters of 2 to 3 from stems in leaf axils. Plant is fragrant. Found in shrubby or open woods areas.

The plant is used as a tea and a coffee substitute, and as a diuretic. Roots were sometimes used to make a purple dye.

False Solomon Seal

39

Fringecup *(Tellima grandiflora)*
One or more stems, 18 to 40 inches tall, with basal leaf clusters. Roundish leaves 1 to 4 inches across, with shallow, toothed lobes, stems long and hairy. White or red flowers on long, slender stem with nodding appearance, all on one side of stalk. Fringed petals, turned back from enlarged calyx, bloom April to June. Found on stream banks or moist, coniferous forests.

Skagit boiled the plant and drank the liquid to help restore a flagging appetite.

Garlic Mustard *(Alliaria officinalis)*
Introduced pot herb. Modified heart-shaped leaf. Small white flower. Found in sun or shade. Herb and seeds may be used for many things.

Used as antiscorbutic, diuretic and expectorant. Also used in salads, sauces and as filler for meat sandwiches. In Wales it is fried with bacon. Good for digestion in humans; bad for cows which, after eating the herb, produce milk with disagreeable flavor.

Monkey Flower *(Mimulus guttatus)*
Leaves ovate; succulent, hollow, squarish stems. Plant grows to 3 feet tall. Bright yellow flower, lower lip marked with crimson or maroon. Blooms May to September. Annual or perennial. Commonly grows in seepage.

Known by natives as "cool water grass".

Pig-a-back or **Youth on Age** *(Tolmeia menziesii)*
Small buds at base of leaf blades develop aerial "daughter" plants. Stem 2 feet tall or taller. Small, drab flowers, purple to brown. Prefers shady, moist, woodland soil.

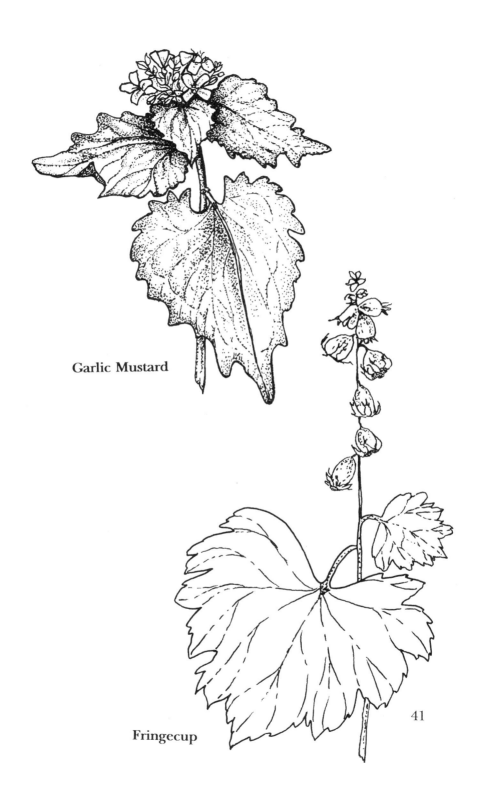

Garlic Mustard

Fringecup

41

Makah ate raw sprouts in spring. Cowlitz applied fresh leaves to a boil.

Queen Ann's Lace or Wild Carrot *(Daucus carota)*
Lacy carrot foliage. Ancestor of domestic carrot. Blooms in late summer and early fall. White umbels, purple center flower. Common in sunny spots. In seed stage, dry tufts ripen to resemble small bird's nest.

Seeds were used for a stimulant, a laxative or a diuretic. Seeds were also used for ulcers and as an agent to regulate blood sugar level.

Self-heal *(Prunella vulgaris)*
Leafy upright shoots. Up to 6 inches tall. Weedy mint; square stem. Perennial, creeps underground. Leaves opposite. Short purple flower. Lower lip of corolla shorter than the upper.

Tea good for gargle, medication for boils; astringent; antispasmodic tonic.

Star-flowered False Solomon's Seal *(Smilacina stellata)*)
Grows to 18 inches tall. Narrow, oval, shiny leaves grow to 6 inches long. White flowers grow in zig-zag plume of about 20 flowers, 1/4 inch wide, 6-pointed star flowers in March to July. Berries a little under 1/2 inch in diameter start green with bluish streaks but ripen to red or dark blue. Commonly found in moist woods.

Young shoots were eaten raw or cooked. Berries edible and high in Vitamin C. Blackfeet people used dried, powdered root to stop bleeding.

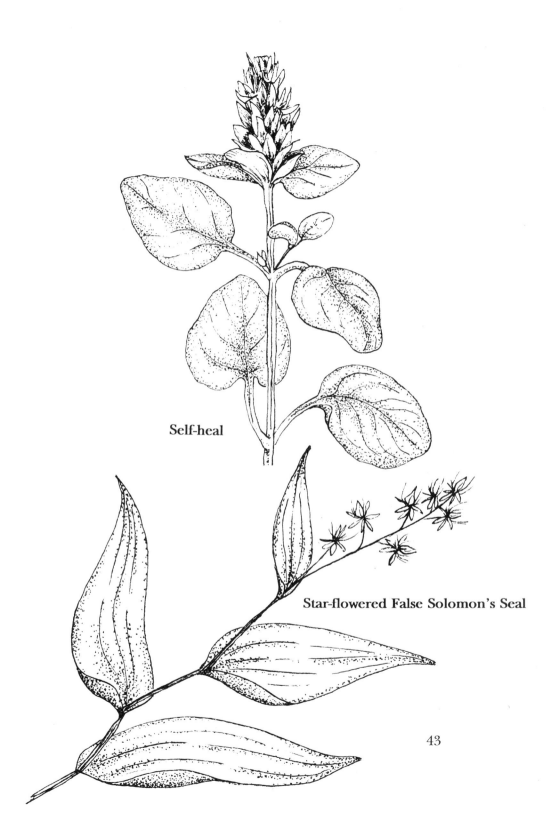

Self-heal

Star-flowered False Solomon's Seal

43

Stinging Nettle *(Urtica dioica)*
Hardy plant, sometimes growing to 5 feet. Underside of leaves studded with hollow, stinging hairs containing small glands filled with liquid formic acid. Contact causes temporary condition similar to an ant bite.

Young plants, when boiled, provided substitute for spinach. Older plants with string-like fibres provided native tribes cordage material.

Trillium *(Trillium ovatum)*
Leaves oval and pointed. Three leaves, 3 petals, 3 sepals. Stalk 12 to 18 inches tall. Color of flower changes from white to rose to burgundy as it dies down. Comes back white again the next year. Blooms late February to April.

Natives used juice from bulb for eye wash. Cooked bulb for a love potion, emetic and female disorders.

Vanilla Leaf, Sweet-after-death or **May Leaf** *(Achlys triphylla)*
Single large leaf on 12 inch stem. Small white flower. Found in open areas where mist and rain temper the sun on the coast. Inland shade preferred.

Cowlitz and Skagit used the leaves in an infusion for tuberculosis.

Waterleaf *(Hydrophyllum tenuipes)*
Few large pinnately compound leaves with fernlike segments. Calyx lobes have bristly hairs along margins. White corolla shading to purple. Flowers in clusters at tips of long stalks. Good ground cover. Blooms May to August. Common in moist open spaces.

Cowlitz broke up and ate root.

44

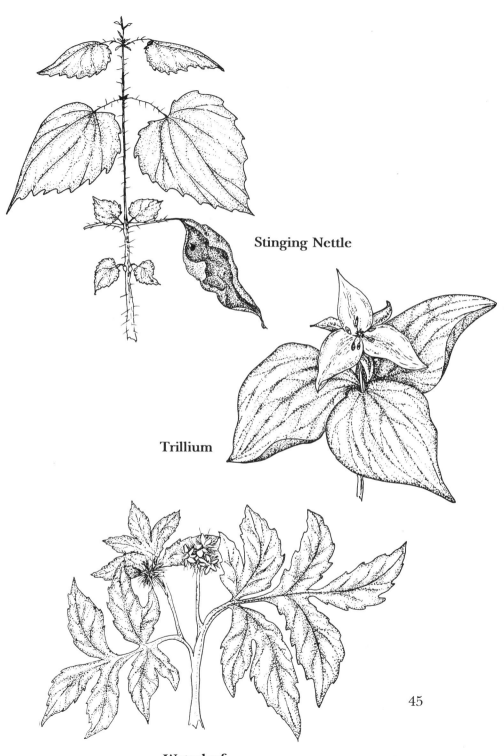

Stinging Nettle

Trillium

Waterleaf

45

Western Buttercup *(Ranunculus occidentalis)*
Several erect, hairy stems growing 4 to 18 inches tall. Hairy leaves, deeply divided into wedge-shaped lobes which are lobed and toothed even further. Basal leaves larger than stem leaves. Deep yellow flowers, about 1/2 to 3/4 inches across, with 5 petals and beaked seed-fruits curved slightly backwards at tip. Found in open areas that are wet in spring and winter but dry in summer.

Cowlitz made a tea for tuberculosis. They recommended a small dose in order not to burn the stomach. Raw plant is poisonous, but toxin is said to be destroyed by drying or cooking. Native people of Rocky mountains boiled and ate roots and made bread meal from seeds.

Western Clematis or **Virgin's Bower** *(Clematis ligusticifolia)*
Tough vine that can climb many feet into trees. Opposite leaves with 5 to 7 leaflets, oval or heart-shaped, 3 inches long with toothed edges. Cream flowers about 3/4 inch wide bloom May to September, with 5 petal-like sepals, no petals and either stamens-only or ovaries-only. Fruit is a silvery plume, 1 to 2 inches long, growing from a seed-type base. Found along stream beds.

The bark was used for sore throat and fever. Poultices were applied to burns. Paiutes made shampoo from the roots. Leaves and stems of plant were turned into a cold remedy when chewed. There are poisonous species also.

Wild Ginger *(Asarum caudatum)*
Leaves heart-shaped; plant hugs the ground to accommodate its pollinators–slugs, ants, millipedes, flies and ground beetles. Flower dark red to purple, a color not seen by bees. Odor of ginger from the whole plant. Found in moist shady woods. This is not the ginger used in cooking. (Commercial

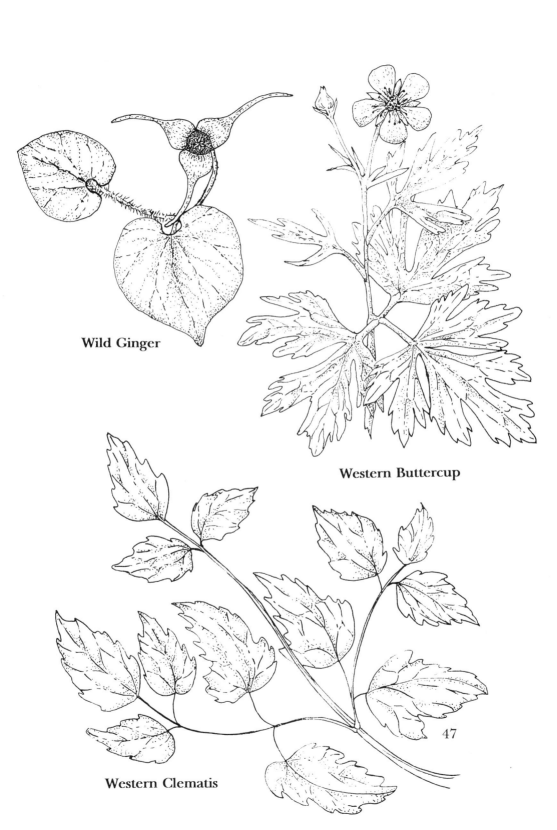

Wild Ginger

Western Buttercup

Western Clematis

47

ginger comes from the root of Zingeber found in Asian tropics.)

Upper Skagit boiled root for tea. Dried leaves were used to treat tuberculosis.

Wild Iris *(Iris tenax)*
One to 4 narrow leaves and 2 purplish leaves shield the buds. Ranges in color from white, cream, yellow to blue and purple. Lives in coniferous or oak forests.

Native people used the plant for making ropes.

Wood Violet or Johnny-jump-up *(Viola glabella)*
Heart-shaped leaves with serrated edges. Yellow flower with marking on lower petal to guide the bees in for nectar. Common in light shade in moist, open woods.

Used as food in Europe. In Denmark, the viola was found in stomach contents of a man's body preserved for 2,000 years.

Yellow Avens *(Geum macrophyllum)*
Leafy plant with one or more stems that can grow to 3 feet in height, although usually about half that size. Basal leaves are long, compound, growing to 1 foot long, end leaflet larger than side ones. Leaves on flower stalk smaller and usually divided into 3 lobes. Yellow flower 1/2 inch wide has 5 downward-turned pointed sepals and 5 broad, 1/4 inch-long petals. Many stamens and pistils with a basal hook and an end that drops off. Seed-like fruit grow many to a head and are hooked at tip. Found mostly in moist woods and meadows.

The plant was used for an astringent. Snohomish and Quileute put the leaves on boils. Quinault smashed the

48

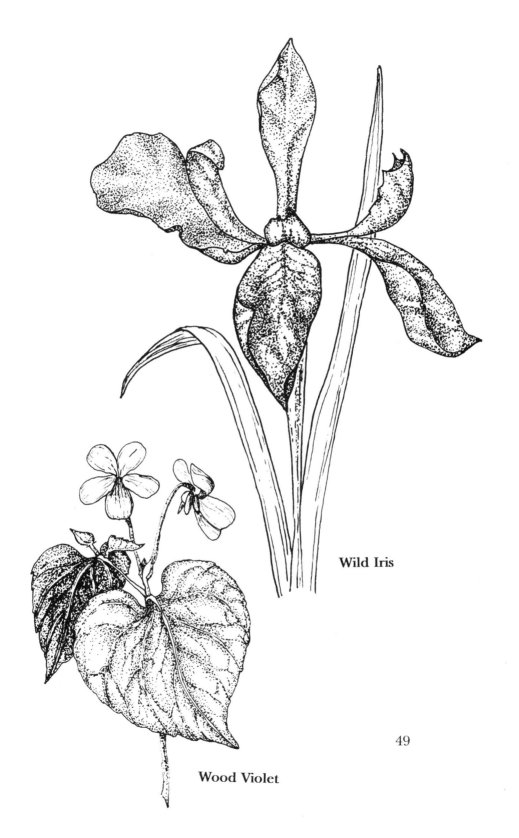

Wild Iris

Wood Violet

49

leaves and placed them on open cuts. Leaves were chewed during childbirth. Chehalis used it as tea to avoid conception.

Yellow Skunk Cabbage *(Lysichitum americanum)*
Strong-smelling, swamp plant with yellow spathes that spring up in dark swamps during February or March. Spathes unfold to reveal spadix, a thick stalk bearing hundreds of small, greenish flowers. Short, fleshy, oval leaves reach up to 56 inches long and 29 inches wide.

Related to <u>taro</u>, staple food of the Polynesians. Islanders roasted and dried roots to quell stinging and burning taste in the mouth. Also could be ground into an edible flour.

A Trinity of Trillium

The lily of threes
in petals, leaves, and sepals
has made a shrine
in an arching niche
of vine maple.

So purely white at first,
then aging in roseate changes
before bleeding to burgundy,
it falls into itself.
Its leaves grow old.

–Anita Hamm

Yellow Skunk Cabbage

CONIFEROUS TREES

Douglas-fir *(Pseudotsuga menziesii)*
Grows to 6 feet in diameter and heights of 250 feet. Needles 1/2 to 1-1/2 inch long grow from branch in bottle-brush style and, although pointed, are soft to touch. Douglas-fir easily recognized by cones. Three-pointed bracts lick out between scales like little tongues or pitchforks. Bark of mature Douglas-fir is dark brown and deeply grooved. Only the redwood grows faster. Grows abundantly throughout Northwest and has been planted elsewhere with success.
Deer and small mammals eat seedlings of this tree; small rodents and birds eat the seeds.

Native Northwest peoples used all parts for medicinal, food and magical purposes. Today it produces more timber products than other trees.

Grand Fir *(Abies grandis)*
Grand fir commonly grows to heights of 200 feet and a diameter of nearly 4 feet. Needles arranged in two flattened rows as if pressed by a book. Cones, 2 to 4 inches long, sit upright on upper branches of tree. Seeds and scales drop individually with core of cone staying on tree. Bark is gray or light brown, becomes more ridged with age. Commonly lives in shaded, moist forests near streambeds. Tends to mingle with other conifers rather than form pure stands.

Fir needles are rich in Vitamin C and were used by native peoples to treat colds. Pitch was used to treat external injuries.

Western Hemlock *(Tsuga heterophylla)*
Grows to 3-1/2 feet in diameter and 200 feet in height. Recognized by its tip, which droops. Needles, very flat, thin and white on underside. Bark, mottled gray and brown.

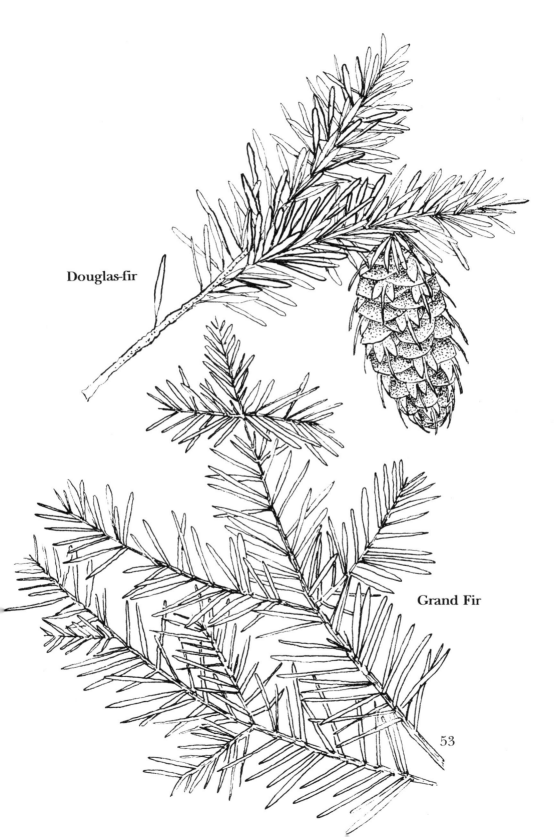

Douglas-fir

Grand Fir

53

Cones, generally 3/4 to 1 inch long and hang downward from branches. A shade-dweller.

Inner bark makes good emergency food. Some Northwest tribes used parts medicinally, and bark, which is high in tannin, was used to dye wood and fishnets.

Western Redcedar *(Thuja plicata)*

Grows to heights of 200 feet and up to 7 feet in diameter. Flat, lacy, slightly yellowish-green leaves. Bark, reddish-brown and peels away easily in strips. Cones, 1/2 inch long, consist of three pairs of seed-bearing scales. Grows in moist spots, especially in fog belts along the coast.

An important plant to some Northwest native people. Every part of the tree had a medicinal use, and some tribes used it in ceremonies. Some used the bark for clothing, diapers, sanitary napkins, and cradle lining. Wood was used for canoes, totem poles, and building timbers. Today, commonly used as timber for shingles, fencing, and boats.

"Trees spring our breath into being, giving it in lttle sips. They scatter shade and literally hold the mountains together."

–Kim Stafford

54

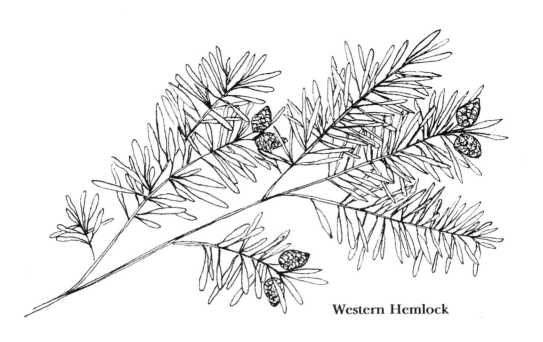

Western Hemlock

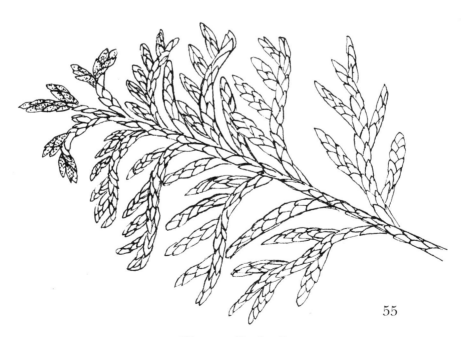

55

Western Redcedar

DECIDUOUS TREES

Bigleaf Maple *(Acer macrophyllum)*
Grows to diameters of 2-1/2 feet and heights of 60 feet or more. Leaf usually 6 to 12 inches wide but sometimes gets as big as 15 inches. Resembles a human hand with fingers outspread. Small green-yellow flowers hang in long bunches visible in spring. Occasionally, bunches can be 4 feet in length. Bark is gray-brown and relatively smooth, when tree is young, and gets grooved as tree reaches maturity. Hairy seeds are paired to form a "V". Prefers rich soil of valleys and foothills and is most common shade tree in Oregon. Produces huge crop of seeds which feed birds and squirrels.

Some Northwest tribes used leaves to line cooking pits. Wood is excellent for flooring and in making instruments and furniture.

Oregon Ash *(Fraxinus latifolia)*
Grows 70 to 80 feet high. Broad, oval compound leaves grow opposite each other. Thick twigs, always opposite at each branch, show clearly when branches are bare. Bark is crisscrossed with ridges and resembles a closely woven net. Likes areas of plentiful moisture and is a lowland plant.

Some Northwest and California native people used bark and root medicinally. Wood is used for baseball bats, oars, arrows, and skis. Wood of young trees better than that of old ones.

Pacific Dogwood *(Cornus nuttallii)*
Grows 20 to 30 feet high. Bright green leaves are pointed, wavy-edged and grow opposite of each other; about 3 to 5 inches long. In Fall, foliage runs from green to orange, red and purple. During flowering season it has the most brilliant white blossoms in the forest. Flowers are small, but

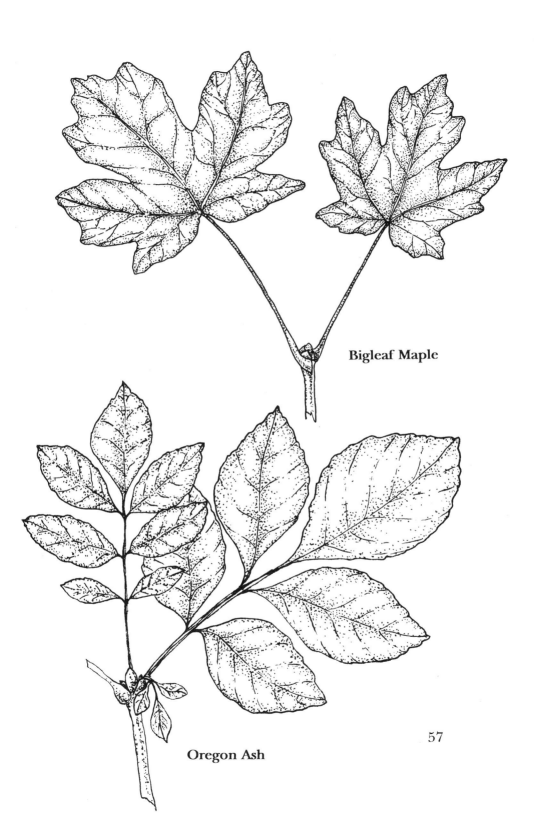

Bigleaf Maple

Oregon Ash

57

have large petal-like scales or bracts. Berries are bright red. Opposite branching and symmetrical appearance of twigs help in identification. Mostly found in low elevation forests west of Cascades.

Bark was used locally as a substitute for quinine. Wood has been used for salmon spears and bows.

Red Alder *(Alnus rubra)*
Fast growing, tree up to 2 feet in diameter and heights of over 100 feet. Reaches old age in 50 to 60 years. Large, blunt leaves; green on top and grayish on underside. Male and female flowers or "catkins" grow on same tree. Female catkins are 1/2 to 1 inch long and resemble small spruce cones. Trunk is gray-white; tiny scale-like lichens growing on bark add whiteness. Grows well on soil with few nutrients. Considered "pioneer" plant.

Some Northwest tribes used wood for utensils and burned it to smoke salmon. They also used wood and bark to make reddish dye. Wood is valued for furniture, paneling, and cabinets.

Vine Maple *(Acer circinatum)*
Survives in heavy shade but seldom grows taller than 25 feet. Leaves are shaped like pinwheels. Flowers, which grow in small clusters, are small and reddish in color. Seed wings (samara) take shape of canoe. Stems are like vines and are red in color. No other tree or shrub in Northwest woods equals its glowing fall colors. When timber trees are logged it often takes over best tree-growing land. Elk and deer like to browse on leaves.

Quinault tribe used long shoots to make baskets.

58

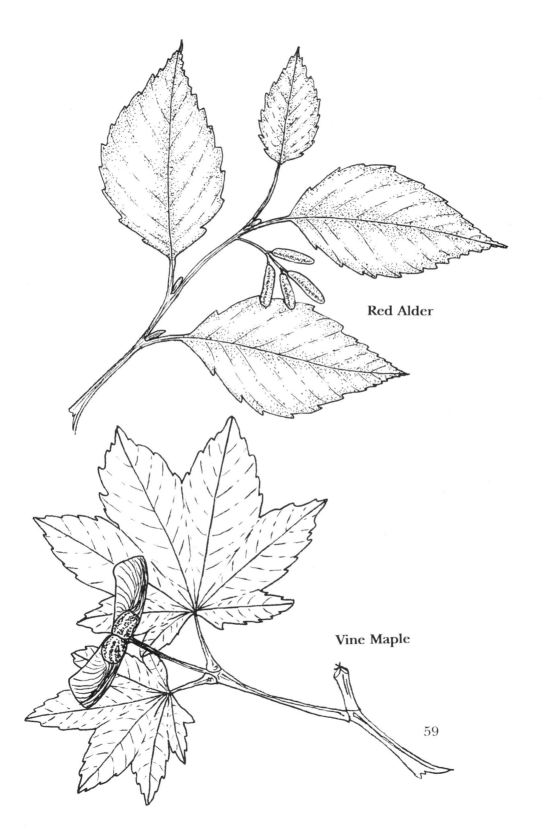

Red Alder

Vine Maple

59

SHRUBS

Indian Plum *(Oemleria cerasiformis* or *Osmaronia cerasiformis)*
Shrub or small tree grows to 15 feet. Leaves 1-1/2 to 3 inches long, slightly oval, smooth-edged. First foliage to appear in spring, bright green turning darker. White flowers, in heavy racemes, have 1/4 inch petals. Drupes, which start yellow, ripen to blue-black. A favorite food of birds. Common along roadsides and low elevation forests.

Berries are edible but bitter-tasting.

Ninebark *(Physocarpus capitatus)*
Shrub, straggly and erect, grows 4 to 12 feet tall. Broad oval, usually 3-lobed toothed leaves 1-1/4 to 3 inches. Reddish bark flakes away in layers. Small white flowers grow in round heads 1 to 2 inches across. Common in moist sites west of Cascades.

Oceanspray *(Holodiscus discolor)*
Shrub grows 3 to 12 feet tall. Oval leaves, 1-1/2 to 4 inches, green and smooth on top, whitish and hairy underneath. Tiny white flowers grow in a cone-shaped cluster, 4 to 7 inches long. One seed grows in dry pod. Common in dry areas.

Native people fire-hardened the wood for a variety of uses.

Oregon Grape *(Berberis nervosa)*
This species not the state flower. Leaves glossy, mildly prickled, veined, and sinewy. Yellow flowers, woody stem. Low-growing ground cover with decorative foliage. Lives among rocks in sunny spots. Also grows in dense shade. Dark blue berries in June.

60

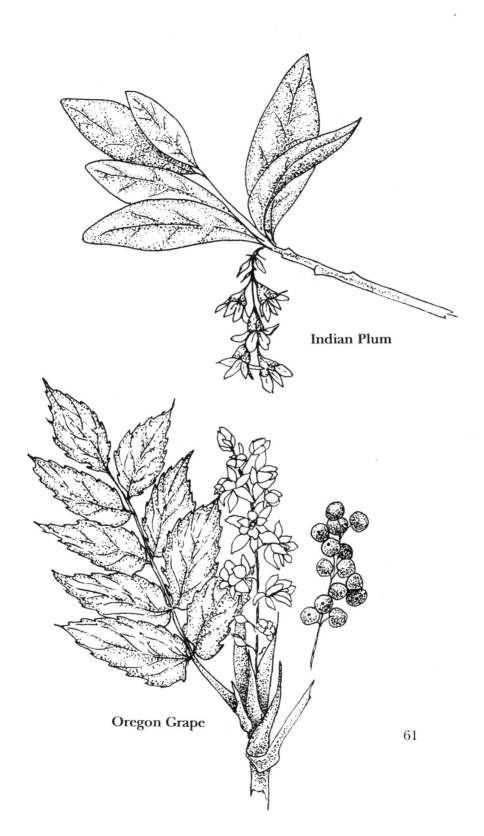

Indian Plum

Oregon Grape

61

Upper Skagit ate berries; boiled roots for venereal disease. Berries were eaten with salmon; the mixture was called "Pemmican".

Poison Oak *(Rhus diversiloba)*
NOT FOUND ALONG PARK TRAILS. Plant favors dry, open areas. Spindly shrub or vine with shiny leaves in groups of three. Small, yellow-green flowers, followed by white berries in late summer. Leaves turn red in fall.

Red Elderberry *(Sambucus racemosa arborescens)*
Shrub or shrub-like tree grows to 20 feet. Opposite leaves, with 5 or 7 leaflets, grow 4 to 12 inches long, pointed with fine-toothed edges. Tiny cream-white flowers grow in dense clusters on racemes with one central stem. Berries, 1/4 inch round with up to 5 seeds, are bright red. Commonly found in clearings west of the Cascades.

Berries are edible but bitter.

Salal *(Gaultheria shallon)*
Sturdy evergreen foliage, height 2 to 4 feet. Leathery ovate leaves, glossy green. Long one-sided raceme. Rose-colored flowers in bells. Fruit, blackish blue, appears in June.

Native people ate the berries in whale oil. The leaves were chewed and spat out for burns and boils.

Salmonberry *(Rubus spectabilis)*
Erect shrub growing 3 to 10 inches tall. Leaves have 3 lobes, 1 to 3 inches long, slightly pointed with sharp-toothed edges. Stems weak and sparsely thorned, with shredding reddish bark. Flowers red to hot pink grow singly or in groups of 2 to 3. Berries are raspberry-like but are yellow to bright red in color. Salmonberry likes wet streambanks and marshes to grow in.

Poison Oak

Red Elderberry

Salal

63

Native peoples of the Northwest used salmonberries to make pemmican with salmon. Green shoots were eaten with salmon to cut the taste.

Snowberry *(Symphoricarpos albus)*
Shrub grows 2-1/2 to 7 feet tall. Oval 1 inch leaves grow in opposite pairs with pale underside. White/pinkish, 1/4 inch flowers. Pure white, 2-seeded berries grow in dense clusters. Taste makes them inedible for humans. Birds and rodents like to eat these, and they disseminate the seeds. Common along roadsides and sparsely canopied areas, often with wild rose and spiraea.

Thimbleberry *(Rubus parviflorus)*
Erect shrub grows 3 to 7 feet tall. Leaves palmate and 5-lobed, very soft with ragged toothed edges, grow up to 8 inches across. Thornless stems are slightly woody but weak. Flowers, white, almost round, 1/2 to 2 inches wide. Edible berries are red, thimble or raspberry-shaped and sweet. Thimbleberry very commonly grows in clearcuts, roadsides and burns.

"True that a plant may not think; neither will the profoundest of men ever put forth a flower."

–Donald Culross Peattie

64

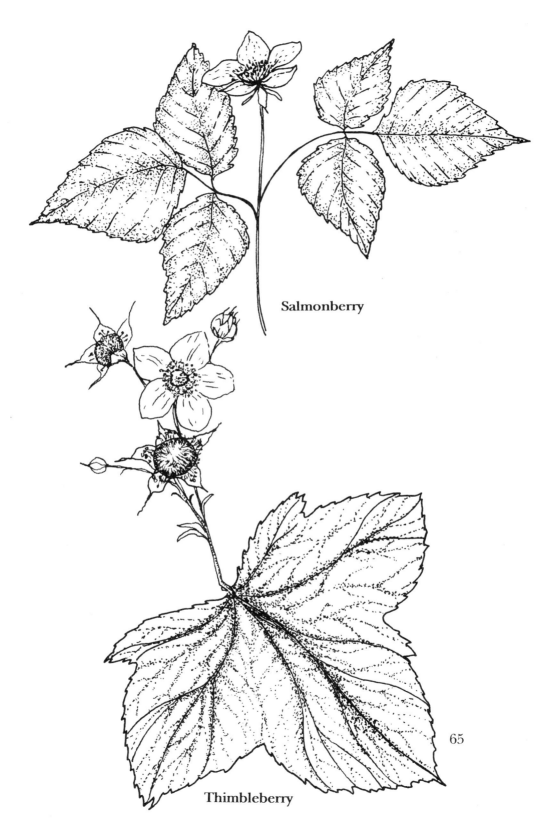

Salmonberry

Thimbleberry

65

GRASSES

In later Spring or early Summer, Tryon Creek State Park's small meadow, located about 1/2 mile south of the entrance road on the bicycle path, produces many grasses.

Grasses *(Gramineae* or *Poaceae Family)* have jointed stems, leaves composed of the sheath and the blade, flowers arranged in spikelets, and fruit consisting of a seedlike grain. Most grasses in the park came from Europe via ballasts in ships or in the straw and hay used as packing materials. Grasses can be identified after they have flowered and gone to seed.

Colonial Bentgrass *(Agrostis tenius)*
Similar to Creeping Bentgrass. Spreads by short rootstalks and rhizomes. Panicles open most of the season. Also known as Common Bentgrass.

Creeping Bentgrass *(Agrostis stolonifera)*
Perennial, 8 to 20 inches tall, with panicle closed most of season and open only when blooming. Leaf ligule thin, 1/32 to 1/8 inch long. Grows from stolons creeping and rooting along the ground's surface.

Orchardgrass *(Dactylis glomerata)*
Perennial, grows in large tussocks, with stems up to 4 feet tall. Roughened blades are 1/8 to 1/2 inch wide, and broadly linear. Sheaths flattened and keeled. Spikelets crowded in dense, single-sided clusters at ends of branches. Widely cultivated for pastures and as hay. Uncultivated, found along roadsides and disturbed habitats. Also known as cock's foot.

Reed Canarygrass *(Phalaris arundinacea)*
Stout perennial with stems 2 to 7 feet tall. Waxy coating gives it a blue-green color. Leaf blades flat, 1/2 to 3/4 inches wide. Panicle initially compact, spreading branches later in season. Found on along streams, and in marshes. Aggressive species. Growth in canals, irrigation ditches, and wetlands creates problems.

Sweet Vernal *(Anthoxanthum odoratum)*
Perennial, growing 8 to 24 inches tall, with slender, erect stems. Spikelets brownish green, and panicles 1 to 5 inches long. Heavy, strong, sweet smell characterizes this plant. Occasionally cultivated as a meadow grass.

Tall Fescue *(Fetusca arundinacea)*
Long-lived perennial with seed stalks up to 4 feet tall. Few to several flowered spikelets. Numerous leaves, stiff, and dark green. Panicles 4 to 12 inches long. Cultivated as a seed and forage crop. Also found on roadsides and in waste places.

Velvetgrass *(Holcus lantus)*
Perennial, growing up to 3 feet tall, with closely clustered stems. Grayish plant, with velvet-like hairs along erect, 12 to 24 inch, stems. Long, narrow, contracted, purple-tinged panicles. Small, curved, hook-like awn, found at second floret of each spikelet. Originally cultivated as a meadow grass, abundantly introduced on the Pacific Coast. Also known as Yorkshire-fog.

HORSETAILS AND FERNS

Horsetail *(Equisetum hyemale)*
Fertile shoots with stems 3/8 inch thick. Cones are 3/4 to 1-1/4 inch long. Reproduces both sexually and vegetatively. Coarse plant with 10 or 12 ridges. It is full of silica. Sometimes called "fern allies". Shoots hollow-jointed, stems bright green, and whorled branches. Found along open road sides, banks, waste land, and seepage. Ancient plant.

Cowlitz washed vermin-infested hair with a decoction of the plant. Good as astringent, tonic, or diuretic.

Bracken Fern *(Pteridium aquilinum)*
A coarse fern, 2 to 6 feet tall. The name "brake" or bracken comes from the broken appearance after a heavy frost. Young green shoots are preferred food of elk and deer, but mature bracken can be poisonous. Bracken is most abundant and largest in the Cascades and westward.

Native people of this area dug up the rootstocks (rhizomes) and roasted them for a starchy food. Today, the young shoots serve as food in several countries. Hunters often use the fern to make a soft bed.

Lady Fern *(Athyrium filix-femina)*
A large, graceful fern 2 to 5 feet high, clear green color in spring. Not evergreen. Sometimes called a swamp fern. Leaves are widest near the middle and taper evenly toward top and bottom. Lowest leaflets very short. Fruit bodies (sori) are gathered in dots on underside of leaflets. Found abundantly throughout the Northwest, along streams and in damp, shady woods.

Lady fern has been used since medieval times to ease labor in childbirth and for a variety of internal maladies.

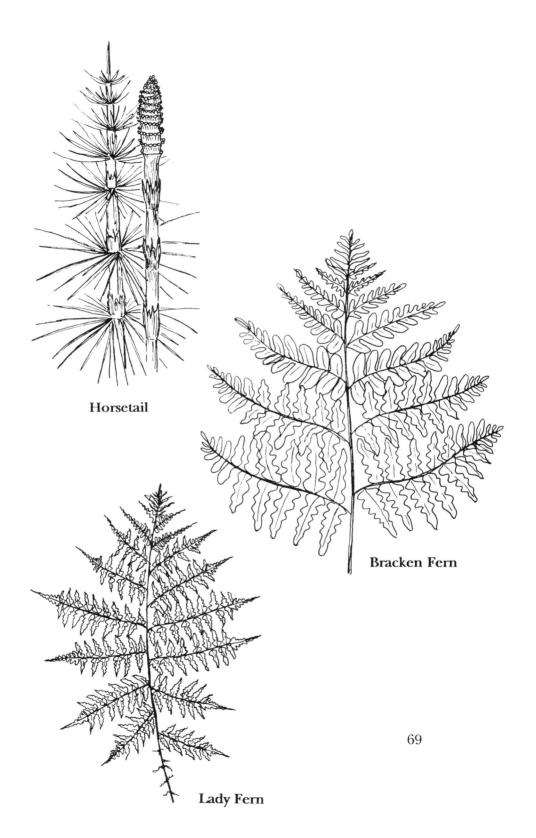

Horsetail

Bracken Fern

Lady Fern

69

Licorice Fern *(Polypodium glycyrrhiza)*
Leaves are 4 to 32 inches long, lobes of leaf may join the midrib in a zig-zag pattern. Ferns grow out of thick moss cover on maples and alders. The sori are large, in rows that are parallel with the midrib of the leaflet. During dry periods it may wither but reappear after the rainy season and remain green all winter. Sparse fern that likes humid conditions.

Its roots have a licorice flavor and were used by native people and settlers to make remedies for various ailments.

Maidenhair Fern *(Adiantum pedatum)*
A delicate fern unlike any other. Soft, thin leaf blades have fringed leaflets along upper edge. Black, shiny leaf stalks or stems in a circular mass. Commonly 1 foot high, produces new leaves all summer. Grows in shade and moisture and along cut soil banks.

Leaves were used for medicinal purposes, some natives used the black stems in basketry.

Spreading Wood Fern *(Dryopteris austriaca)*
Finely cut, lacy fern has leaves which range from a few inches high to 2 feet or more. Found on bases of trees. Whole leaf has a triangular shape. Sori, when young, covered by circular shield and gathered in dots. Found in moist, shady woods of western Oregon and Washington, especially at low elevations. *Pictured on page 73.*

Both rhizomes and leaves were used medicinally.

Sword Fern *(Polystichum munitum)*
Has evergreen leaves 1 to 5 feet long which rise from central point in circular manner. Name is derived from short,

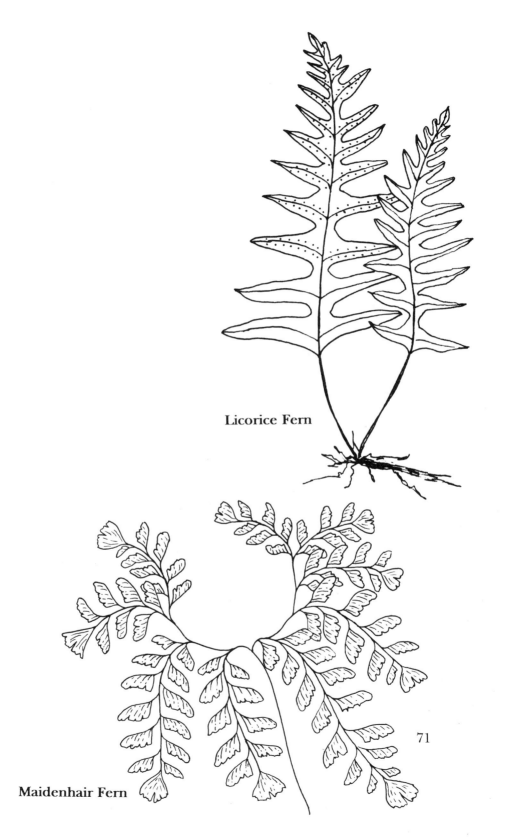

Licorice Fern

71

Maidenhair Fern

broad sword appearance of leaf or frond. Shield-covered fruit cases (sori) are in a row near margin of leaflet, giving the underside of leaves an orange-brown color. This tough, coarse fern is found throughout the Northwest, especially in shade offered by dense growth of fir, hemlock, and spruce.

Had many medicinal uses among the native people and was used for mattress stuffing. Today, this fern is used for making sprays and wreaths.

"...to find the universal elements enough; to find the air and the water exhilarating; to be refreshed by a morning walk or an evening saunter...to be thrilled by the stars at night; to be elated over a bird's nest or a wildflower in spring - these are some of the rewards of the simple life."

–John Burroughs

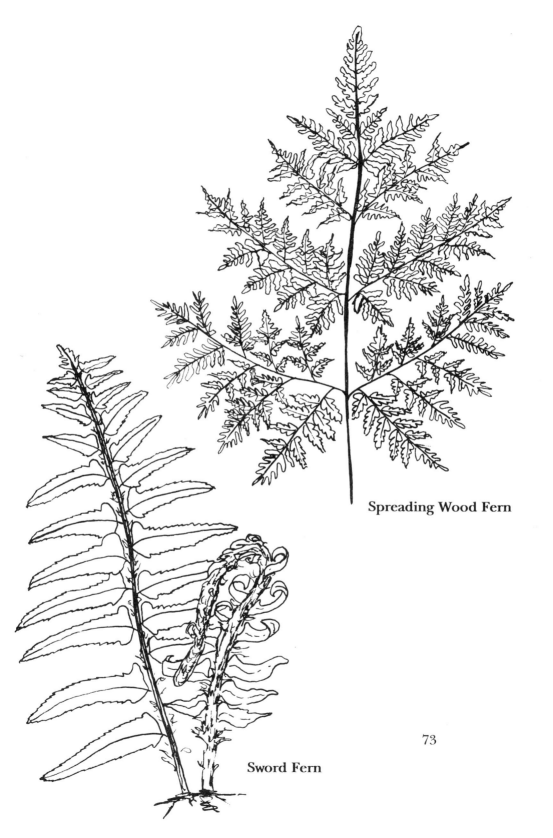

Spreading Wood Fern

Sword Fern

73

MOSSES, LICHENS, AND FUNGI

MOSSES

Mosses were one of the first land plants. Like lichens and fungi, they do not have a vascular system. Their thin leaves have no veins. Instead of roots, they have rhizoids or hair-like tubes. They absorb moisture from the air. As green plants, they make their own food. They are found on trunks and limbs of trees, fallen logs, and on the ground.

Mosses can tolerate extreme climatic conditions. After drought, they will respond to rain to make a comeback. Moss, because of its water-holding ability, prevents erosion on hills and shady places.

Mosses are of two general types:

Upright, erect stems with little or no branching. Examples:

> **Juniper Hair Cap** *(Polytrichum juniperinum)*
> Dull, blue-green with reddish tips. Grows on rocks and logs.

> **Menzies's Tree Moss** *(Leucolepsis menziesii)*
> A tree-like moss, more delicate than the coarse Juniper Hair Cap. A group resembles a stand of tiny palm trees. Grows in wet areas, near streams, on the ground or on decaying logs.

Trailing, prostrate or creeping, freely branching; tend to form thin, flat, tangled mats. Two trailing mosses in the park are:

(Neckera sp.)
Pale green leaves flattened along the stem, with curled waves. Grows on living tree trunks, on limbs, or on rocks.

Oregon Beaked Moss *(Eurhynchium oreganum, E. stokesii)*
A common moss; green to golden, large feather-shaped plant with very fine leaves; found on dead wood and forest debris.

LICHENS

Lichens are a combination of an alga, a microscopic green plant, and a fungus, a non-green plant. In this mutually beneficial partnership, the alga can utilize sunlight and carbon dioxide to make food; the fungus holds water and provides structure. The spores of certain algae and fungi are in the air all the time, and, when they come together in favorable environment, they join to form a new plant or thallus.

Lichens are primitive plants that have no stems, leaves, or roots. Their entire surfaces absorb nutrients from the air. In the park they are found on tree trunks, branches, dead wood, rocks, mosses, or on the soil. There are an abundance of lichens on park trees. They do not harm the trees, which serve only as a point of attachment for the lichens. These plants harbor insects that sustain birds in the winter. Lichens are adaptable, remaining dormant in dry periods and at low temperatures for years, only to revive when conditions are favorable. They act as an indicator of fresh air and will not grow in pollution.

Lichens come in an assortment of colors, ranging from greenish gray, greenish yellow, lemon yellow, orange, brown, tan, and to slate blue.

There are three forms of lichen:

Crustose is tiny, flaky or crusty. Dusty white in circular areas, on the bark of alders and maples.

(Lecanora sp.)

Foliose is papery, resembles lace or leaves and also grows in ruffled mats. Some types of foliose lichens are:

Dog Ear Lichen *(Lobaria pulmonaria)*
Gray-green, lettuce-like, classic lichen.

Golden Xanthoria *(Xanthoria polycarpa)*
Orange, grown in patches

(Hypogymnia sp.)
Flattened, puffy, green above and black beneath.

(Parmelia subaurifera)
Olive brown on twigs

(Parmelia sulcata)
Flat, single thickness attached to branch of twig; green with white ridges above, black below.

Fruticose, or shrubby lichens, grow vertically erect or hanging down from trees. Some examples are:

Old Man's Beard *(Usnea sp.)*
Feathery, gray-green round cords with elastic inside; white to gray on bark of alders.

(Evernia prunastri)
Flat, single-thickness lichen attached loosely to branch or twig; green above and white below.

(Ramalina sp.)
Gray-green above and below.

FUNGI

There are over 240 species of fungi within Tryon Creek State Park's boundaries. The area is small; therefore fungi should not be collected but enjoyed through photography and the natural history walks available in the park.

Honey Mushroom *(Armillariella mellea)*
Although this is a virulent parasite of over 200 species of plants, including rhododendron and poison oak, it is among the most variable and cosmopolitan of the fungi. It can grow on wood or be buried underground. In the mycelial stage, it is called "shoestring root rot". A great edible that should be identified with care.

Strict Coal Mushroom *(Ramaria Stricta)*
This pale yellow or tan-coral fungus is very common on sticks and half-buried fallen twigs. Its presence indicates that the recycling of forest nutrients is underway.

Grisette *(Amanitopsis vaginata)*
There is good evidence that this fungus is rhizomorphic with both conifers and hardwoods. When first emerging from the forest floor, it looks like a hard-boiled egg with a light brown top.

Shaggy Parasol *(Lepiota rachodes)*
The major importance of this fungus is the recycling of compost and leaves of the forest duff. It produces several crops a year. As a safe and edible fungus, Shaggy Parasol adds a tasty element to its function as part of nature's recycling team.

Witches' Wax Cap *(Hygrocybe conica)*
An unusual yellow-orange to black fungus that is solitary on the ground in damp, conifer-wooded areas. Its fruit is most obvious in fall and winter, continuing the recycling of soil mosses and forest floor debris started earlier by soil bacteria. Sometimes it may even occur on lawns.

Plums and Custard *(Tricholomopsis rutilans)*
In the late 19th and early part of this century, many cedar and other conifers were removed from the park area. Remaining stumps are often the food source of this beautiful purple-red scaled fungus with bright yellow gills. The decay process is slow, but, as the wood is being broken down the stump, becomes habitat for *(Dicranum)* mosses, *(Cladonia)* lichens, and *(Scapania)* liverworts.

Train Wrecker *(Lentinus lepidius)*
Bigleaf Maples are often broken in wind and ice storms. This exposes trees to the spores of an eventual brown rot. The scaly cap and serrated gills of this white fungus can sometimes be seen high on the side of both conifers and hardwoods in the fall.

Spring Angel Wing *(Pleurocybella porrigens)*
Every once in a while, an old tree snag falls which has been worked over by woodpeckers, insects, and the spores that produce this interesting oyster-like fruiting body. The fungus appears in the Spring and Fall. The fungus mycelium and bacteria in a number of years reduce the snag to valuable minerals.

Pleated Marasmius *(Marasmius plicatulus)*
With a velvet-red top and a black stem, this is one of the park's prettiest small fungi. It aids in the recycling of conifer and broad-leaf foliage.

Cloudy Clitocybe *(Clitocybe nebularis)*
Up to 10 inches across and gray-white in color, this is one of the largest gilled fungi in the park under the trees. As Fall has just about ended, it fruits in large numbers and smells a little like rancid flour. There is evidence that it is rhizomorphic with both conifers and hardwoods, as the mycelia intertwine with fine rootlets of the forest floor.

"Some live and learn life is for growing
some live and die never knowing."

–Illon M. Sillman

79

MAMMALS

Upwards of 40 species of mammals live in Tryon Creek State Park, but most go unnoticed by visitors. Unlike humans, most park mammals are nocturnal. Mammals also differ from birds, whose colored feathers and colorful songs attract attention. Most mammals are secretive and have fur that tends to blend in with the surrounding vegetation.

Even though mammals may be difficult to see and hear, they play important roles in the forest. Chipmunks and squirrels aid in the dispersal of tree seeds. The tunneling activity of moles turns the soil, increasing aeration and recycling of decaying plant material. Dam building by beavers can alter the plant and animal life in and along Tryon Creek.

The Park as a Wildlife Sanctuary

Prior to pioneer settlement of the Willamette Valley, a wide variety of mammals, large and small, flourished here. The vast forests and riverside meadows provided abundant food and cover. Native peoples supplemented their fish and plant diet with rabbits and deer caught by traps and bow and arrow.

By 1850, Oregon Trail pioneers were starting to farm the meadowlands along the major waterways near the park. The demand for wood increased and, by 1870, logging camps were springing up in the nearby forests. Major logging activity in the park occurred between 1880 and 1920. Prior to this time, large native mammals such as black bear, Roosevelt elk, and mountain lions roamed the forested hills. These animals need large contiguous areas in order to find enough food, and the newly created farmsteads and clearcuts disrupted their habitats. The larger mammals including elk and bear were also hunted for their meat and hides. The hunting pressure and habitat loss forced the remaining large mammals to retreat to the mountain foothills. They are rarely seen on the valley floor today.

Not all mammal populations declined as a result of human activities. Deer and coyotes found the farmland and clearcuts to their liking and have increased in numbers. Raccoons, squirrels, and chipmunks have also increased as the forests returned. Several introduced mammals established themselves in the Portland area. Most notable is the ever-present American Opossum.

Even though established neighborhoods surrounded the park as early as the 1930's, the majority of roads and houses were built in the last 30 years. As remaining properties are further subdivided, wildlife habitat shrinks. The park's forested ravines and creek bottom provides a welcome refuge for many large and small mammals. Even though one may not see or hear them on a visit here, the mammals of Tryon Creek State Park are thriving in this refuge of water and trees.

"What is man without the beasts? If all the beasts were gone, men would die from a great loneliness of the spirit. For whatever happens to the beasts soon happens to man."

–Chief Seattle, 1854

81

MAMMALS IN THE PARK

American Opossum *(Didelphis marsupialis)*
This marsupial, the size of a domestic cat, is easily identified by its pointed face, black ears and feet. It has a long, scaly, naked tail on its grayish body.

Opossums were brought to Oregon from the Southeastern states in the 1940's. Since then, their populations have been increasing in the Portland area. Opossum success can be traced to the fact that these pouched mammals can have several litters per year. Each litter can have as many as 11 young. Very few predators bother to attack opossums and the young that do survive have "cast iron" stomachs, able to consume just about any food. During the day, most opossums rest in trees or dens, and, at night, they roam the forest in search of food. Typical natural fare includes bird eggs, insects, and berries.

Shrews *(Sorex spp.)*
These tiny creatures, no more than 5 inches long, including their tails, have short pointed snouts, small eyes and short legs. Their soft fur ranges in color from dark to light gray or brown.

Shrews are among the most common, but least known, animals in the park. These small hyperactive mammals are busy day and night, in constant search of food for their voracious appetites. Shrews hunt insects and earthworms in the leaf litter and can sometimes be seen scurrying across the trail. Visitors sometimes mistake them for mice.

Townsend Mole *(Scapanus townsendi)*
These 8 to 9 inch long mammals have long, pointed, nearly hairless snouts, and short naked tails. With palms pointed outward, their broad shovel-like feet are armed with strong,

82

American Opossum

Trowbridge Shrew

Townsend Mole

83

flattened nails for digging. Their soft, velvety black fur repels water and soil with ease.

Landscapers and gardeners take a dim view of this common Northwest mammal as its tunneling activities can wreak havoc in a lawn or flower bed. However, in a forest setting, the mole's habits are quite beneficial. Its tunneling activity turns the soil, aerates it, and speeds decay of fallen leaves and twigs. Like shrews, moles have hearty appetites and help keep the earthworm and underground insect population in check. When moles surface from their tunnels, they run the risk of being captured by owls, coyotes, and house cats.

Bats *(Families Vespertilionidae and Molossidae)*
The only true flying mammals, these small creatures fly with wings formed from a membrane of skin stretched between the tail, hind legs, and the extended toe of the fore limbs. They range in size from 3 to 6 inches. Fur colors include many shades of brown and gray.

Several species of bats live in the park. During the day, they roost in tall fir trees and under rock overhangs. At night, bats emerge from their roosts and hunt for mosquitoes and other flying insects, using echolocation (animal sonar) to locate their quarry. When the insect population dwindles in the late fall, bats either hibernate in old buildings or caves or migrate south to warmer locales such as California or Mexico.

Brush Rabbit *(Sylvilagus bachmani)*
Not much more than 12 inches in length, with short legs, this rabbit has a concealing dark brown fur above and a lighter brown below. The white tail so common in other rabbits is barely visible.

84

Little Brown Bat

Brush Rabbit

Rabbits are one of the animals people expect to see when they visit a park. This is usually <u>not</u> the case here at Tryon Creek. The native brush rabbit is very shy and secretive, usually making brief appearances only at dawn and dusk and never very far from the protective cover of a bushy thicket. This animal must be ever alert to predators that would attack it day and night: hawks, coyotes, owls, and dogs. Brush rabbits forage for grasses, berries, and the new growth on many shrubs and ground covers. They may be seen on the edges of the parking lots and along the bike trail.

Douglas Squirrel or **Chickaree** *(Tamiasciurus douglasi)*
Small for a tree squirrel, 12 inches including tail, the chickaree has dark brown or olive-colored fur above with orange or yellowish underparts. Its blackish brown tail is edged with yellow or white.

This noisy squirrel is more often heard than seen. Its bird-like, scolding call greets the visitor who intrudes on its feeding or nesting territory. Douglas squirrels are active here year round, storing Douglas-fir and maple seeds in the summer and fall and digging up these food caches in the winter and early spring. Occasionally, the larger fox squirrel is seen in the park, usually near residential areas where it searches for berries and the fruits of nut-bearing trees. Both of these squirrels are subject to predation by cats as they leave the trees to bury their food supplies.

Northern Flying Squirrel *(Glaucomys sabrinus)*
About 12 inches in length including tail, this expert glider has soft, silky fur, and large dark eyes. Upper parts of the body and tail are dark brown or gray with lighter underparts. A flat tail and fur-covered membranes, stretched between fore and hind limbs, gives this squirrel the ability to maneuver and glide.

86

Douglas Squirrel

87

Northern Flying Squirrel

Rarely appearing before total darkness, flying squirrels emerge from their tree cavity nests and search for food on the forest floor. Fungi make up the bulk of their diets, but seeds and insects are also eaten. These curious mammals can be attracted to bird feeders where they feed on sunflower seeds. Here in the park, flying squirrels must be on constant guard, for their chief predator, the great horned owl, is usually nearby. To stay ahead of this efficient hunter, the squirrel glides quickly and quietly from one feeding area to another.

Townsend Chipmunk *(Eutamias townsendi)*
Approximately 10 inches in length, this large, brown-colored chipmunk has grayish stripes on its back and head. Like the Douglas squirrel, the Townsend chipmunk can be quite vocal. Its call is a shrill "chip-chip".

This is the mammal most often seen by park visitors, either standing on a log or scurrying across the trail. Much of its day is spent searching for seeds, fungi, and small insects. Chipmunk activity picks up in the fall as they store food supplies for the winter. Park chipmunks retreat to their dens during prolonged cold spells, feeding from their stored food caches. Unlike squirrels in some national parks and forests, Tryon Creek chipmunks are wary of people and will usually run away when approached. They can and will bite when cornered.

Beaver *(Castor canadensis)*
This busy rodent, with its broad, flat scale-covered tail and webbed hind feet measures up to 40 inches and weighs between 40 and 50 pounds.

Because its thick fur was so highly prized, the beaver was trapped to near extinction by the late 1800's. Changing

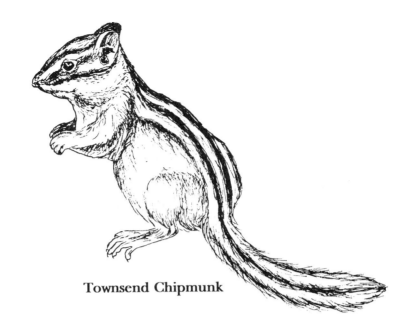

Townsend Chipmunk

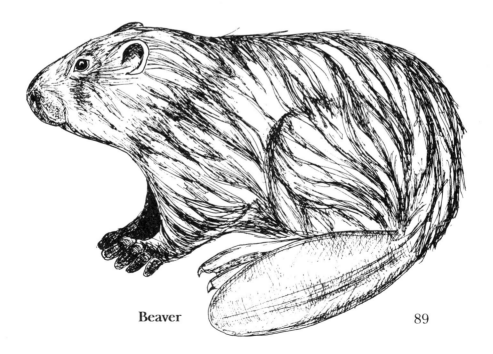

Beaver

89

fashion trends and protection measures have caused beaver populations to increase in recent years.

This largest rodent in the park lives along Tryon Creek. Beaver sightings are rare because the animals are usually active in the evening and early morning hours. Bark and twigs of Red Alder trees are the beaver's primary food here.

The location of beaver activity along the creek changes over the years with the food supply and human activity. The animals may abandon a stretch of stream where dogs are allowed to run and play in the water.

Beavers live in dens they dig into the creek bank - lodges are rarely built by Willamette Valley beavers. Beaver dams are also uncommon here in the park. More reliable evidence of their presence is tracks in the mud, and twigs and branches showing their gnawing activity.

Two beaver look-alikes can be found in waterways near the park. The smaller muskrat has a round tail, and prefers slow moving streams or ponds with marshy vegetation. The South American nutria, slightly smaller than the beaver, with gray fur and a round tail, was introduced to Oregon in the 1930's. It has spread rapidly and can now be found in many sluggish streams, canals and drainage ditches throughout the Willamette Valley.

Mice and **Voles** *(Family Cricetidae)*
Several species of these two groups of rodents live in the park. Deer mice are very common nighttime residents, scurrying under the leaf litter in search of seeds and insects. Voles, also called meadow mice, prefer more open areas and can occasionally be seen along the bike path. Both of these mammals are important food items for hawks, owls, coyotes, and foxes.

90

Deer Mouse

Meadow Vole

91

Coyote *(Canis latrans)*

If seen, the coyote might be mistaken for a slender German Shepherd. They have a graceful, springing gait with the tail held down as they run. Smaller than wolves, coyotes have more pointed muzzles and large pointed ears which face forward. With coloration of light grayish brown and shades of red on legs, feet, and ears, the coyote often blends in with the surrounding rocks and vegetation.

Coyotes have found a home in Tryon Creek State Park. The familiar yipping sounds made by these dog-like mammals can also be heard in the surrounding neighborhoods. The intelligent and adaptable coyote is an opportunist, eating whatever is available at the time. Depending on the season, food items can include mice, insects, and berries. Sometimes coyotes will attack larger prey, including raccoons and even small deer. However, people have no reason to fear these animals. A healthy coyote will keep a safe distance from hikers, runners, and horseback riders.

Red Fox *(Vulpes fulva)*

Approximately 40 inches long with the appearance of a small dog, red foxes usually have reddish yellow fur with white underparts. The tail is tipped with white and its feet are black.

One of the well-established neighborhoods bordering the park is Red Fox Hills. Undoubtedly, this area was named for the foxes that once lived there. It appears that the red fox population in and near the park is on the decline, as fields and old orchards yield to roads and houses. Fox sightings are now infrequent and some of these sightings are probably of the more adaptable and widespread coyote.

The red fox found in the Willamette Valley was brought to Oregon from the Eastern states for sport hunting and fur

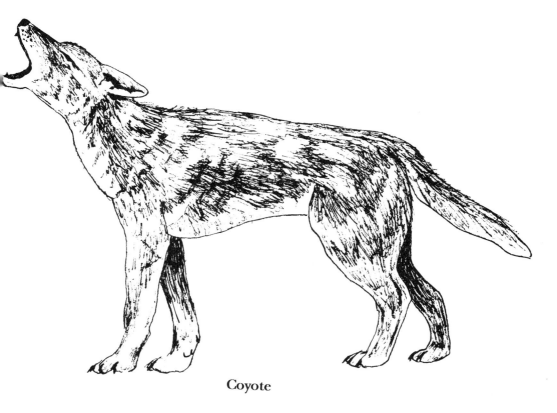

Coyote

Red Fox

93

ranching. The Valley is also home to the gray fox, an Oregon native. The preferred food of both foxes is mice, but they also eat birds, insects, and berries.

Raccoon *(Procyon lotor)*
A black masked face with pointed nose and ears and a black and brown striped tail easily distinguishes this medium sized, 40 inch, mammal.

Most people are familiar with the "masked bandits" of the forest. Portlanders are used to having raccoons prowling their neighborhoods and raiding their trash cans and pet food bowls.

Raccoons prefer to live near a stream or pond where they search for crayfish, salamanders, frogs, and small fish. Raccoons rely on their well-developed sense of touch in their feet and whiskers as they feel for their underwater meals.

The best place to find evidence of raccoons in the park is at the creek. Tracks may be seen in the mud near the bridges.

Striped Skunk *(Mephitis mephitis)*
About the size of a house cat, their shiny, black fur is in sharp contrast to the white stripe which marks the forehead between their button-black eyes. This skunk's white stripe extends from the top of the head, making a "V" down the back to the base of its bushy tail, which also may be tipped or mixed with white.

Skunks are more often smelled than seen, and encounters with them in the park are rare. These nocturnal members of the weasel family search for insects, mice, and birds in the more open areas of the park. Most potential predators, such as coyotes, learn to avoid skunks. The telltale odor drifting through a residential area is often the result of a skunk's

Raccoon

Striped Skunk

close encounter with a dog or cat.

Blacktail Deer *(Odocoileus hemionus)*
This medium sized deer, a subspecies of the Mule Deer
found east of the Cascades, stands 3 1/2 feet tall and may
weigh as much as 200 pounds. Its winter coloration is
grayish, and, in summer, the deer is reddish or buff, with
white throat and rump patches, and a black tail. Large ears
distinguish this animal, which has a bounding gait with its
four feet coming down simultaneously.

A small population of blacktail deer lives in and around the
park. Using ravines as corridors, the deer wander in and out
of the park in search of nutritious vegetation. Favorite foods
include the new growth on Sword Fern, Salal, and Vine
Maple. As growth slows on native plants in the late summer
and fall, deer will seek out flowers and vegetables in nearby
gardens. Here automobiles may suddenly encounter them
on Terwilliger and Boones Ferry Roads.

"The silence of snowy ashes of the forest,
the whirring flight of partridges, the impudent bark
of squirrels, the quavering voices of owls and coons,
the music of the winds in the high trees - all these
impressions unite in my mind like parts of a
woodland symphony.

–Hamlin Garland, (1860-1940) American Writer

Blacktail Deer

BIRDS

More than 60 species of birds spend all or part of the year at the park. Many more are regular or casual visitors who stop to rest and feed in route to their nesting areas in the Spring or to their wintering grounds in Fall. Winter is a fine time to see the park's birds because the maple and alder trees are bare of leaves and the feeders are kept stocked. Spring is the time to learn to distinguish a few of the songs with which the male of each species marks out his family's territory.

A number of the birds described here can be recognized on a single walk. Visit several different habitats such as forest, deciduous woods, streamsides, edges of open fields, parking lots, and where the borders of these habitats meet.

When one sees a bird, one should note as many of the following distinguishing features as one can: size in relation to a common bird (as, larger or smaller than a robin), shape, color, and flight pattern (flapping, soaring, undulating). Any, or all, may be distinctive. Because each species clings to its own ecological "niche" in one or more levels of the forest community, the most useful clue to a bird's identity is often not what it looks like, but how it behaves. Some obvious features of appearance and behavior may help in identifying some of the birds most likely to be seen or heard on a walk through the park.

AROUND THE BIRD FEEDERS

Particular bird species may be found around the Nature Center and on the Trillium Trail:

Band-tailed Pigeon *(Columba fasciata)*
A large, 13 inch, wild pigeon that resembles the rock dove

Band-tailed Pigeon

99

(domestic pigeon) but is heavier and has a distinctive gray tail band and white stripe on the back of the head. Band-tailed pigeons are summer residents that nest here in tall fir trees. Visitors often mistake their "rook-a-roo" call for an owl's hooting.

Chickadees *(Parus atricapillus* and *Parus rufescens)*
Black-capped and Chestnut-backed Chickadees are common bird feeder visitors. The brown back on the Chestnut-backed, distinguishes the two species. They are 4-3/4 to 5-3/4 inches long. They nest in woodpecker holes, and, in winter, roam the forest in small flocks, feeding on seeds and insects. Their call is an unmistakable "chick-a-dee-dee-dee".

Dark-eyed Junco *(Junco hyemalis)*
A small, 5 inch, ground feeding bird which shows distinctive white outer tail feathers when flying. Juncos gather in small flocks to feed on fallen conifer seeds; formerly called Oregon Junco. Call is a ringing metallic trill.

Pine Siskin *(Carduelis pinus)*
A goldfinch-like bird with brown-streaked and yellow tinted plumage, 4-1/4" to 5-1/4 inch, often seen in large flocks looking for seeds. Pine siskins will wander over large distances, so time spent in one area is often brief. Call is scratchy "teee and schhrree".

Red-breasted Nuthatch *(Sitta canadensis)*
A small, 4-1/2 inch, white and blue-gray tree climber who searches tree trunks and branches for insects by climbing downward, head first. Often seen at bird feeders with chickadees. Call is a nasal "yank yank".

Rufous Hummingbird *(Selasphorus rufus)*
Small, 3 to 4 inch bird common to mixed forest edges. Male has rufous upper body, bright red-orange gorget and white

Black-capped Chickadee

Dark-eyed Junco

Pine Siskin

101

Red-breasted Nuthatch

breast. Female is green with rufous coloring on sides and under tail. Usually lays 2 eggs in nicely constructed nest made of and mosses and lichens. Low buzzy call. Visits Nature Center hummingbird feeders.

Rufous-sided Towhee *(Pipilo erythrophthalmus)*
A ground-feeding bird, 7 to 8-1/2 inches, with black back, rusty red sides, white breast, and red eye. Rufous-sided towhees are found in the underbrush, scratching for seeds and insects using a backward kicking motion. Call is "meewww?".

Song Sparrow *(Melospiza melodia)*
A small, 5 to 7 inch, brown bird with whitish breast streaked in brown with a central breast spot and long, rounded tail. This common bird's musical song often begins with two or three short notes followed by trills.

Steller's Jay *(Cyanocitta stelleri)*
A 12 to 13-1/2 inch blue colored jay with a black crest, common in coniferous forests. Bold and raucous, Steller's jays are regular visitors to the bird feeders, often chasing off chipmunks and Douglas squirrels. Their call is a series of "Shack, chook" sounds. *Pictured on page 105.*

Varied Thrush *(Ixoreus naevius)*
A robin-like bird, 9 to 10 inches, with a black breast band. Often seen along with robins in residential areas in winter, the varied thrush spends its summers in the nearby mountains. It searches the forest floor for insects, seeds and berries. Call is a soft buzz and "took". *Pictured on page 105.*

Rufous Hummingbird

Song Sparrow

Rufous-sided Towhee

103

IN THE TREES AND SHRUBS

Many birds rarely if ever visit the bird feeders. These elusive birds may be found in the trees and brush along the trails:

American Robin *(Turdus migratorius)*
Red-breasted, 9 to 11 inches long. Less visible in the forest than in residential areas. All are highly territorial during the nesting season. Feeds on earthworms, insects, fruit and is very fond of cherries and crabapples. Call is "cheer-up, cheerily".

Cedar Waxwing *(Bombycilla cedrorum)*
A small, 6 inch, crested bird with red wing spots and yellow tail tip. Flies in small flocks searching for berries of trees and ornamental shrubs. Often seen in residential areas surrounding the park. Call is high "see-e-e-e".

Cooper's Hawk *(Accipiter cooperi)*
Sharp-shinned Hawk *(Accipiter striatus)*
Both of these forest-dwelling hawks are identified by their short, rounded wings and long tails. They fly from secluded branches to catch small birds. The Cooper's hawk is larger, 14 to 20 inches, than the Sharp-shinned, 10 to 14 inches, but their similar coloration make it difficult to separate them. Call is "kek, kek, kek".

Kinglet *(Regulus calendula* and *Regulus satrapa)*
Very tiny, 3 to 4 inches, olive-gray birds with red or yellow head patches. Ruby-crowned distinguished from golden-crowned by incomplete eye-ring. Kinglets are most visible in winter when they fly in loose flocks searching for insects in fir branches. Calls are high pitched "see-see-see" notes.

Varied Thrush

Steller's Jay

Cooper's Hawk

105

Townsend's Warbler *(Dendroica townsendi)*
Hermit Warbler *(Dendroica occidentalis)*
Bright colored active little, 4 inch, birds that flit through the trees in constant search for insects. Many are migratory and are usually seen passing through the park. Most western Oregon warblers have yellowish markings on their throats, wings or breast feathers. Townsend's call is a "wheezy, wheezy, wheezy, twee or dee", while the Hermit's call is a soft "chup".

Winter Wren *(Troglodytes troglodytes)*
A tiny, 3-1/4 inch, brown bird with a short "trimmed off" tail. The winter wren feeds on insects in low brush, often beside the trail. From February on, its song can be heard, which is a series of high clear trills, rising and falling for a full five seconds.

WOODPECKERS

The park and surrounding neighborhoods are prime woodpecker habitat. This is because dead trees are allowed to stand and decay in place. Small insects seek out these snags for food and shelter. Woodpeckers search out these trees for the same reasons. Woodpeckers in the park are:

Downy Woodpecker *(Picoides pubescens)*
Hairy Woodpecker *(Picoides villosus)*
Small to medium sized, 7 to 10 inches, black and white woodpeckers often seen searching for insects on tree trunksand branches. Males of both species have red spot on back of head. Downy call, a soft "pik"; Hairy, a loud "peek".

Northern Flicker *(Colaptes auratus)*
Large, 11 inch woodpecker with long bill, spotted black and buff breast, and brick red coloring under the wings. Its rhythmic, dipping flight is characteristic of most

Downy Woodpecker

Pileated Woodpecker

107

Winter Wren

woodpeckers, but, unlike other species, the flicker spends much time on the ground searching for ants and berries.

Pileated Woodpecker *(Dryocopus pileatus)*
Very large, 16 to 19-1/2 inch, woodpecker of black and white plumage with a showy red crest. Probes for insects and larvae in dead snags, leaving large oblong holes (other woodpeckers make round ones). Very loud "kak, kak, kak" call and drumming can be heard for quite a distance. *Pictured on page 107.*

DOWN BY THE CREEK

The lack of ponds and large marshy areas keeps large numbers of ducks, geese, and shorebirds from visiting the park. However, several birds do find food and refuge in and near water.

Belted Kingfisher *(Megaceryle alcyon)*
A large-headed bird, 11 to 14 inches, with a bushy blue crest and spear-shaped bill, about 11 to 14 inches in size. As its name implies, the kingfisher feeds primarily on small fish. It may be seen flying along the creek just above the water or perched on a dead snag watching for movement below the water surface. The kingfisher call is a loud rattle.

Great Blue Heron *(Ardea herodias)*
A long-legged wading bird, up to 4 feet tall, with a long dagger-like beak used to spear small fish, frogs, and crayfish.Color varies from pale gray to medium blue. This stately bird may be found wading in Tryon creek near the bridges. The official "City bird" of Portland. It has a loud "grak" or "kraak" call.

Northern Flicker

Belted Kingfisher

Great Blue Heron

109

Mallard Duck *(Anas platyrhynchos)*
This common duck can be seen swimming in quiet stretches of the creek. The green head of the male mallard is unmistakable. The female is a dull brown color. Both are about 20 to 28 inches. Mallards here may be wild birds or refugees from local parks and golf courses.

INTO THE NIGHT

Most birds are active during the day (diurnal). However, a large group of birds flies by night. Two members of this nocturnal group, owls, are common in the park and surrounding areas:

Great Horned Owl *(Bubo virginianus)*
A large, 20 inch, owl of forest and field, the Great Horned owl lives throughout the Willamette Valley. In this area, it feeds primarily on mice, rabbits and flying squirrels. Horned owls are often called "hoot owls" because they make a "hoo, a-hoo, a-hoo" call at night.

Western Screech Owl *(Otus kennicotti)*
This small, 8 inch owl with ear tufts is common in the Portland area. It nests in abandoned woodpecker holes and hunts mice. Unlike other owls which have hoot-like calls, the screech owl often whistles and trills.

Great Horned Owl

111

Western Screech Owl

AMPHIBIANS AND REPTILES

Most animals in Tryon Creek State Park go unnoticed by the majority of visitors. Many small animals carry out their lives under the dense cover of vegetation on the forest floor and are rarely seen. Others venture out only under the cover of darkness. Still others live in habitats that are difficult for humans to reach, such as under ground and along the creek bottom. These are the realms of the park's amphibians and reptiles.

AMPHIBIANS

Amphibians are well represented here in the park. The mild, damp conditions in the forest and along the creek are ideal for frogs and salamanders. These animals have smooth, moist skin that would quickly dehydrate in drier habitats. Also, frogs and salamanders breathe with gills sometime during their lives, and must remain close to water or very damp soil to complete their life cycles. The other main group of amphibians in Oregon, the toads, are usually found in drier habitats.

SALAMANDERS

Rough-skinned Newt *(Taricha granulosa)*
This distinctive salamander is characterized by its warty, brown back and sides, and orange belly. Breeding (aquatic) males, however, are smooth-skinned. These salamanders are often encountered on land in forested areas near water. Breeding in the park occurs in spring and early summer. The animals have a striking warning display in which the tail is arched well over the back. *Pictured on page 115.*

Northwestern Salamander *(Ambystoma gracile)*
This salamander is 5 to 8 inches long and uniformly brownish above. The large parotid gland behind each eye and a noticeable ridge along the upper edge of the tail are good field marks. Northwestern salamanders are usually found along stream banks in moist forests. These animals are secretive and may be difficult to find.

Long-toed Salamander *(Ambystoma macrodactylum)*
This common, slender salamander is distinguished by a stripe down its back and by its long slender toes. Long-toed salamanders are most often found in the spring when nearly any body of standing water may serve as a breeding pond. These animals seem to have no rigid habitat requirements and can appear in grasslands as well as in the forest.

Pacific Giant Salamander *(Dicamptodon ensatus)*
The largest (8 to 11 inches) salamander in the park, this formidable-looking animal has a mottled color pattern and a large head. It is usually found near water under logs and rocks but can occasionally be seen crawling across the trails. These salamanders breed in clear cold streams, and the larvae may live in the creek several years before becoming an adult salamander.

Ensatina *(Ensatina eschscholtzi)*
This large, brown salamander can be identified by the constriction at the base of its tail and the light color at the end of its legs. Ensatinas are often found as they travel over the forest floor. They hide in stumps, logs, and the burrows of small mammals. Their warning display is to stand stiff-legged with the back arched down and the tail arched up.

FROGS

Red-legged Frog *(Rana aurora)*
This is the largest native frog, though the non-native bullfrog may be several times larger. Red-legged frogs have prominent folds on the body and a reddish color on the lower abdomen and underside of the thighs. They appear near permanent ponds and in damp woods. Eggs are laid in ponds in the spring. Once common in suitable habitat in the Willamette Valley, this frog now seems to be found only infrequently, perhaps a result of predation by bullfrogs.

Bullfrog *(Rana catesbeiana)*
This introduced frog has an eardrum as large or larger than its eye. Bullfrogs may be found in any body of water that has enough vegetation to provide adequate cover. Their tadpoles take two years to develop into adult frogs. Sounds made by adults include the deep, resonant "Jug-o-rum" of breeding males, and a high-pitched "erk" when alarmed frogs leap for water. These frogs eat nearly any live food they can catch, including insects, other frogs, small turtles, and even mice and bats. They may be serious predators on native amphibians and reptiles.

Pacific Tree Frog *(Hyla regilla)*
The color of this small frog varies widely, but they usually have a dark stripe through each eye. The finger and toe tips end in large pads which enable tree frogs to be excellent climbers. They are common throughout the Willamette Valley. Breeding occurs in the spring but males may begin to call from ponds during warm weather even in early January.

114

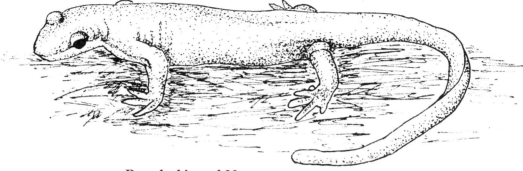

Rough-skinned Newt

Pacific Tree Frog

115

TOADS

Western Toad *(Bufo boreas)*
This is the only native toad. It is easily distinguished by its squat, compact body, and greenish-brown, warty skin. Western toads occur in a variety of moist and wet habitats, but in this area are usually found in or near forests. The animals usually live in burrows which they dig themselves.

REPTILES

In the Northwest, reptiles are represented by the turtles, snakes, and lizards. Even though all three groups are found in the Willamette Valley, snakes and lizards are more common in the drier eastern and southern sections of the state. The dry, scaly skin of reptiles enables them to survive in drier, more open habitats than the amphibians. Reptiles breathe with lungs. Therefore, they are not confined to wet or damp locations as amphibians must be.

TURTLES

Painted Turtle *(Chrysemys picta)*
This is the most widely distributed turtle in North America. It occurs in lakes, ponds, and slow-moving streams. These turtles often bask on logs or on shore. Painted turtles have distinct yellow lines on their head, neck, and forelegs and a red margin on the shell.

SNAKES

Ringneck Snake *(Diadophis punctatus)*
One of the most attractive snakes, this species is easily recognized by its red-orange neckband and belly. Ringnecks are secretive but occur in a variety of moist habitats, usually with abundant logs and rocks under which they may hide.

When threatened, a ringneck hides its head and displays the red underside of the coiled tail. If handled, ringnecks are gentle but discharge a foul smelling liquid, a behavior they share with garter snakes.

Common Garter Snake *(Thamnophis sirtalis)*
This is the most widely distributed snake in North America and is commonly found here near water and in other wet habitats. The regularly spaced red blotches on the sides are distinctive. Common garter snakes give birth to their young and feed on frogs, salamanders, fish, worms, and mice. These snakes are active daytime hunters and so may be encountered on a walk in the park. They may bite and will almost certainly discharge a foul smelling substance if handled. They readily take to water and swim very well.

Western Rattlesnake *(Crotalus viridis)*
NOT FOUND IN THE PARK. This species is the only snake in Oregon potentially dangerous to humans. Its rattle is distinctive, as is the heat sensitive pit between each nostril and eye. Although western rattlesnakes appear near Salem, southward in the Willamette Valley, and east of the Cascades, they are not to be expected in the Portland area.

Northwestern Garter Snake *(Thamnophis ordinoides)*
This is the common garter snake in the area. It appears in woods, meadows, vacant lots, yards and gardens. Northwestern garter snakes are so highly variable in color pattern as to give the impression that one must be dealing with several different species! They feed on many kinds of invertebrates including slugs, frogs, and salamanders. Garter snakes are usually the first snakes to be seen in the spring, when they bask in sunny areas near cover. *Pictured on 119.*

Rubber Boa *(Charina bottae)*

As the name suggests, this snake somewhat resembles a piece of rubber hose. The head and tail are about the same size and there is an "eye spot" on each side of the tail. When threatened, these snakes tend to form a coil with the head at the bottom and the tail up and waving about. These gentle, beneficial snakes are nocturnal and spend much of their time in burrows, leaf litter, and under logs in damp forests. Rubber boas feed on small invertebrates, such as worms and insects, which are killed by constriction. These snakes give birth to their young, as do the common garter snake and the western rattlesnake.

"The snake's eyelids close upon its jeweled eyes. It sloughs off its skin with delicate design. It sleeps quietly in the water's ooze, waiting for sun to warm the rocks."

–Anita Hamm

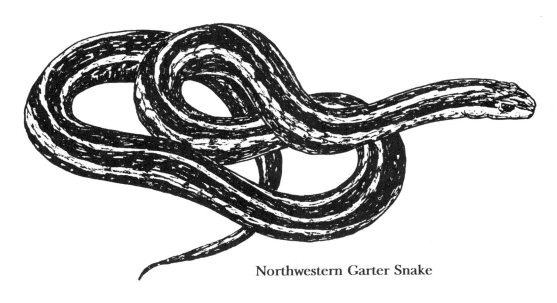

Northwestern Garter Snake

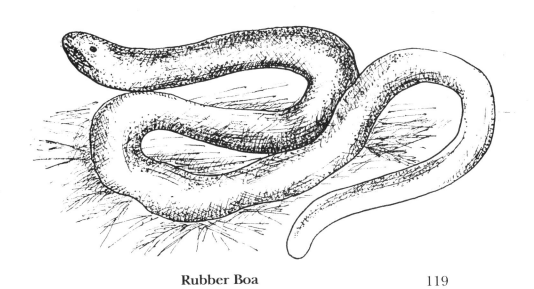

Rubber Boa   119

ARTHROPODS

Most of the animal life in the park has not been listed or described in this book. There are dozens of species of insects and spiders as well as aquatic insects and soil inhabiting "bugs". Arthropods, animals with articulated bodies and limbs, include some very large groups including the insects, arachnids (spiders), and crustaceans (sowbugs, crayfish).

INSECTS

Bees and **Wasps**
Several species live in the park. Noteworthy are the bald-faced hornets that build large paper nests on tree limbs. Also, there are ground-nesting bees at work in the summer. These insects vigorously defend their nests and a hiker walking off the trail could be in for a painful surprise.

Butterflies and **Moths**
There are colorful swallowtail butterflies near the creek, where they are attracted to streamside flowering plants. The black and red caterpillar of the Isabella moth, better known as the woollybear, can be seen crawling across park trails in the fall. Other noteworthy insects appearing in the late summer and fall, are the tent caterpillars and fall webworms. These caterpillars spin silk tents around tree branches as they feed on the leaves. The adults of both species are small moths.

Mosquitoes
Mosquitoes are most abundant here from early May through July. They are an important food source for small birds and bats.

120

Dragonflies and Damselflies
These flying insects can be found at the creek. The adults eat smaller flying insects that they catch on the wing. Damselflies are usually smaller and more delicate, often with a bluish body color. Adult dragonflies are larger and are faster fliers. The larvae live a quite different life clinging to the underside of rocks and twigs in the creek. They are an important food source for herons and fish.

Beetles
Several species of beetles can be seen crawling across park trails. Some feed on mushrooms and other plant material; others are predators that catch smaller insects. A common park beetle is the ground beetle of which several species live here. These 1-inch long, black beetles are active mainly at night. During the day they often hide under logs and stumps but can sometimes be seen crawling across the trails.

Spittlebugs
In late Spring, a white froth appears on the stems of trailside plants. Spittlebugs make this froth to cover their eggs and to hide in while they are feeding on the plant. Birds and other predators are likely to overlook them in this protective cover.

Carpenter Ants
These common household pests are important to the health of the forest. Their tunneling in logs and stumps helps to break down the wood into soil. The 1/2 inch workers, which are wingless females, are eagerly sought out by woodpeckers and other insect eating birds.

OTHER ARTHROPODS

Spiders
Many species of spiders live in the park. All are predators, feeding on small insects or other spiders. Early-morning joggers have the unpleasant task of breaking through spider webs built across the trails during the previous night. Spiders set these web "nets" to catch flying insects. Other spiders live on the ground and in flowers, where they lie in wait and ambush small insects that venture too close. Spiders are a favorite food item for many park animals including birds, salamanders, and shrews.

Centipedes and Millipedes
These common arthropods live on the forest floor. The brown-colored, inch-long centipedes are predators chasing down slower moving prey. They are active at night but can be seen, during the day, hiding under rotting stumps and logs. Millipedes can be seen crawling across park trails on rainy days. Black with red spots, these many-legged arthropods feed on decaying plant material.

Pillbugs and Sowbugs
These are related to lobsters and crayfish. These small, 1/2 inch, land crustaceans live under leaves and logs and feed on decaying plant material and fungi.

Crayfish or Crawfish
A freshwater relative of the lobster, crayfish crawl along the bottom of Tryon Creek searching for a meal of small fish, aquatic insects, or bits of decaying plant material. They, in turn, are food for raccoons and herons.

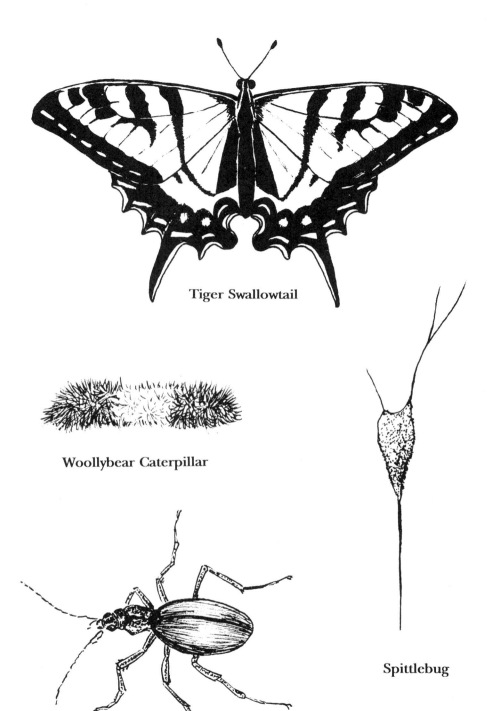

Tiger Swallowtail

Woollybear Caterpillar

Spittlebug

Ground Beetle

123

MOLLUSKS

Slugs and Snails

The banana slug is one of the most frequently seen animals in the park. This "snail without a shell" crawls about in search of mosses, lichens, and fungi. Mushrooms are also a favorite food. The mucous slime, covering the slug, prevents it from drying out and deters some predators from eating it. However, opossums, raccoons, and salamanders will eat slugs on occasion.

Snails can also be seen in the park. They have similar diets and habits as the slugs. Certain snails have brightly colored shells. These shells offer some protection from predators, and the snail can also withdraw into the shell to escape hot, dry weather.

"It is interesting to contemplate an entangled bank, clothed with many plants of many kinds, with birds singing on the bushes, with various insects flitting about, and with worms crawling through the damp earth, and to reflect that these elaborately constructed forms, so different from each other, and dependent on each other in so complex a manner, have all been produced by laws acting around us.

–Charles Darwin

Snail

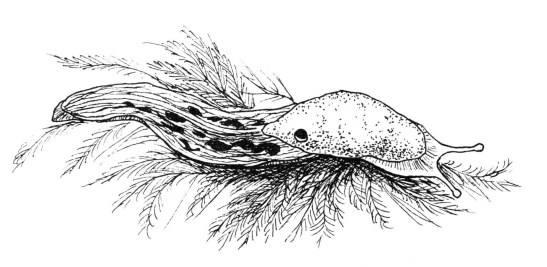

Banana Slug

THE TRAIL SYSTEM

Tryon Creek State Park has more than 14 miles of maintained trails that serve a variety of users. The trails provide access to the forest and the creek and allow visitors to experience nature close up and close in. Most park trails were built, during the 1970's, by dedicated volunteers, and they continue to help maintain these trails today.

Here is an introduction to the park's trail system. A trail map, which includes suggested walks, is located elsewhere in this book.

THE TRAILS

Bicycle Path
The 3-mile, paved, bicycle path runs parallel along Terwilliger Boulevard on the east edge of the park from Boones Ferry Road to State Street (Highway 43) in Lake Oswego. It is part of the Portland metropolitan bikeway system and the 40-mile Loop.

Equestrian Trails
The horse trails have the greatest variation in grade. Each begins near the ridgeline and travels down to the creek and back. The trail surface is packed gravel, which can support horse traffic and is passable even in wet weather. Horse trailer parking is available near the Nature Center.

North Horse Loop (2.1 miles)
Begins in the equestrian parking area next to the Nature Center. It is also the starting point for the park Volkswalk.

West Horse Loop (1 mile)
Begins at High bridge and forms a "figure eight"
loop with the North Horse Loop.

Boones Ferry Horse Trail (.35 miles)
Englewood Horse Trail (.47 miles)
Both trails are connectors from residential areas to
the West Horse Loop. No horse trailer parking is
available at these trailheads.

The Trillium Trail (.35 miles)
This barrier-free trail is designed for people of all abilities.
It has paved pathways, drinking fountains, resting benches,
and viewing decks. Features of the trail are identified along
the way.

Nature Center Trails
These three trails are the most popular in the park. They
surround the Nature Center and view the canyon. They
have a slight elevation change and are maintained for year-
round hiking. Woodchips cover them to allow for
comfortable and quiet walks.

Maple Ridge Trail (.62 miles)
A forest fire around the turn of the century opened
the forest along this trail to allow a number of maple
trees to grow. Many visitors find this trail a prime
location for identifying a number of plants found in
the park.

Center Trail (.49 miles)
This trail, located between the Maple Ridge and Big
Fir trails provides the least elevation change of the
three.

Big Fir Trail (.59 miles)
A nice stand of fir trees can be found along this trail, offering visitors the feel of being in a wilderness not too far from home.

Park Trails
More than 5 miles of non-paved trails reach into most sections of the park and provide an opportunity to experience the many park environments, from forest to creek.

Old Main Trail (.55 miles)
Built by the Civilian Conservation Corps in the 1930's as a connector trail between the Dunthorpe and Englewood neighborhoods, Old Main is the most heavily used park trail. It begins at the Nature Center, crosses Obie's bridge, and connects to the West Horse Loop.

Middle Creek Trail (.56 miles)
This trail connects the Nature Center trails to the creek. Two bridges, High and Beaver, are located along this scenic trail.

Cedar Trail (.96 miles)
This challenging trail meanders through side ravines on the west side of the park. There is a lot of up and down hiking and, during wet weather, muddy conditions.

Iron Mountain Trail (1.1 miles)
This hiking trail, the longest in the park, used to be an old logging road. Stone bridge, an interesting arched stone and concrete structure, spans a small tributary stream along this trail. Also on this trail is the Iron Mountain Bridge.

Red Fox Trail (.41 miles)
Named for the neighborhood in Lake Oswego where the trail begins/ends, the Red Fox trail contains the only set of tight switchbacks found along park trails. The Red Fox Bridge, located on this trail, crosses Tryon Creek.

South Creek Trail (.37 miles)
This trail parallels Tryon Creek and connects the Red Fox and Iron Mountain trails.

Lewis and Clark Trail (.86 miles)
The principle hiking trail in the north end of the park is named after the college and not the explorers. Hikers using this trail can connect to the North Horse Loop and the bike path.

Fourth Avenue Trail (.12 miles)
This is a short trail that connects the 4th Avenue residential area with the Lewis and Clark trail.

Hemlock Trail (.11 miles)
Another short connector, this trail links the Englewood Horse trail with the Cedar trail.

North Creek Trail (.44 miles)
One can follow Tryon Creek north of High bridge to Boones Ferry Road on this trail. It is a less-used but muddy alternative to the Boones Ferry Horse trail.

"What we love...when we step into the coolness of a wood, is that its boughs close up behind us. We are escaped into another room of life."

–Donald Culross Peattie

Tryon Creek Volkswalk

The park is host to a year-round volksmarch, or "folk walk". These non-competitive walks, held in several state parks, are sponsored by the Oregon Trail State Volkssport Association and the Oregon Parks and Recreation Department. The Tryon Creek Volkswalk is an 11 kilometer (7 mile) route that makes use of sections of the bike path, equestrian trails, hiking trails, and streets in a Lake Oswego residential area.

"To enjoy scenery you should ramble amidst it; let the feelings to which it gives rise mingle with other thoughts; look round upon it in intervals of reading; and not go to it as one goes to see the lions fed at a fair. The beautiful is not to be stared at, but to be lived with."

–Thomas Babington Macauley, (1800-1859) English Writer and Statesman

CHECKLISTS

PLANTS OF TRYON CREEK STATE PARK

Ground Covers and Wildflowers

___ Alum Root *(Heuchera micrantha)*		white
___ Aster, Douglas *(Aster douglasii)*		purple
___ Avens, Yellow *(Geum macrophyllum)*		yellow
___ Baneberry; China Berry *(Actaea rubra)*		white
___ Bedstraw, Cleavers *(Galium aparine)*		white
___ Bedstraw, Fragrant *(Galium triflorum)*		white
___ Bishop's Cap *(Mitella caulescens)*		green
___ Bitter Cress *(Cardamine pulcherrima)*		white
___ Bleeding Heart, Pacific *(Dicentra formosa)*		pink
___ Bunchberry, Canada Dogwood *(Cornus canadensis)*		white
___ Burdock *(Arctium minus)*		green/white
___ Buttercup, Creeping *(Ranunculus flammula)*		yellow
___ Buttercup, Little *(Ranunculus uncinatus)*		yellow
___ Candy Flower, Siberian Miner's Lettuce *(Montia sibirica)*		pink
___ Chickweed *(Stellaria media)*		white
___ Chicory, Blue Sailors *(Cichorium intybus)*		blue
___ Clover, Red *(Trifolium Pratense)*		red
___ Clover, White *(Trifolium repens)*		white
___ Colt's Foot *(Petasites frigidus)*		white
___ Columbine, Red *(Aquilegia formosa)*		coral
___ Compass Plant *(Sylphium lacinatum)*		yellow
___ Cow Parsnip *(Heracleum lanatum)*		green
___ Cucumber, Wild *(Marah oreganus)*		white
___ Dandelion *(Taraxacum officinale)*		yellow
___ Dock, Western *(Rumex occidentalis)*		green
___ Dogbane, Spreading *(Apocynum androsaemifolium)*		pink
___ Duckfoot; Inside-out Flower *(Vancouveria hexandra)*		white
___ Evening Primrose *(Oenothera biennis)*		yellow
___ Fairy Bells, Hooker *(Disporum hookeri)*		white
___ False Dandelion, Cat's Ear *(Agoseris glauca)*		blue/green
___ False Hellebore *(Veratrum californicum)*		green/white
___ False Solomon's Seal *(Smilacina racemosa)*		white
___ False Solomon's Seal, Star-flowered *(Smilacina stellata)*		white

Ground Covers and Wildflowers continued

___ Fireweed *(Epilobium angustifolium)*	rose
___ Foxglove *(Digitalis purpurea)*	purple
___ Fringecup, *(Tellima, grandiflorum)*	white/pink
___ Garlic Mustard *(Alliaria officinalis)*	white
___ Geranium, Cut-leaf *(Geranium dissectum)*	pink
___ Ground Ivy, Creeping Charlie *(Glecoma hederacea)*	blue
___ Groundsel, Ragwort *(Senecio vulgaris)*	yellow
___ Hawkbit, Fall Dandelion *(Leontodon autumnalis)*	yellow
___ Hawkbit, Hairy *(Leontodon nudicaulis)*	yellow
___ Hawksbeard, Rough *(Crepis occ)*	yellow
___ Heal-All *(Prunella vulgaris)*	violet
___ Hedge Nettle *(Stachys cooleyae)*	purple
___ Honesty; Money Plant *(Lunaria annua)*	pink
___ Horsetail, Common *(Equisetum arvense)*	green
___ Indian Pipe *(Monotropa uniflora)*	white
___ Iris, Wild *(Iris tenax)*	purple
___ Knotweed *(Polygonum aviculare)*	green
___ Knotweed, Japanese *(Polygonum cuspidatum)*	white
___ Lemon Balm *(Melissa officinalis)*	white
___ Lily-of-the-Valley, False *(Maianthemum dilatatum)*	white
___ Miner's Lettuce *(Montia perfoliata)*	white
___ Monkey Flower *(Mimulus guttatus)*	yellow
___ Mustard, Field *(Brassica campestris)*	yellow
___ Nightshade, Enchanter's *(Circeae alpina)*	white
___ Orchid, Phantom *(Eburophyton austiniae)*	white
___ Oxalis, Oregon *(Oxalis oregana)*	white/yellow
___ Oxalis, W. Yellow *(Oxalis suksdorfii)*	yellow
___ Ox-eye Daisy *(Chrysanthemum leucanthemum)*	white
___ Pathfinder, Silver/green *(Adenocaulon bicolor)*	white
___ Pearly Everlasting, Anathalis *(Anaphalis margaritacea)*	white
___ Periwinkle, Phlox *(Phlox adsurgens)*	pink/blue
___ Pig-a-back, Youth on Age *(Tolmeia menziesii)*	purple
___ Pineapple weed *(Matricaria matricarioides)*	yellow
___ Plantain *(Plantago major)*	green
___ Poison Hemlock *(Conium maculatum)*	white
___ Queen Ann's Lace; Wild Carrot *(Daucus carota)*	white
___ Self-heal *(Prunella vulgaris)*	purple
___ Sheep Sorrel, Sour Grass *(Rumex acetosella)*	red

Ground Covers and Wildflowers continued

___ Skunk Cabbage, Yellow *(Lysichitum americanum)*	yellow
___ Snowberry, Waxberry *(Symphoricarpos albus)*	pink
___ Sour Grass *(Rumex acetosella)*	red
___ Speedwell, American *(Veronica americana)*	blue
___ Spring Beauty, *(Cardamine pulcherrima)*	lavender
___ St. John's Wort, *(Hypericum perforatum)*	yellow
___ Starflower, Western Broad-Leaved *(Trientalis latifolia)*	yellow
___ Starwort *(Trientalis arctica)*	white
___ Stinging Nettle *(Urtica dioica)*	green
___ Strawberry, Wood *(Fragaria vesca)*	white
___ Sweet Cicely, Western *(Osmorhiza chilensis)*	white
___ Tansy Ragwort *(Senecio jacobaea)*	yellow
___ Teasel *(Dipsacus sylvestris)*	purple
___ Thistle, Canada *(Cirsium arvense)*	purple
___ Thistle, Common *(Cirsium vulgare)*	purple
___ Tiger Lily, Columbia Lily *(Lilium columbianum)*	orange
___ Trillium, Western Wake Robin *(Trillium ovatum)*	white
___ Twinflower *(Linnaea borealis)*	pink
___ Twisted Stalk, White mandarin *(Streptopus amplexifolius)*	white
___ Vanilla Leaf, Sweet-after-Death *(Achlys triphylla)*	white
___ Vetch, American *(Vicia americana)*	purple
___ Violet, Evergreen *(Viola sempervirens)*	purple
___ Water Parsley *(Oenanthe sarmentosa)*	white
___ Waterleaf, Pacific *(Hydrophyllum tenuipes)*	purple/white
___ Western Buttercup *(Ranunculus occidentalis)*	yellow
___ Wild Ginger, Western *(Asarum caudatum)*	dark red
___ Wood Sorrel, Western Yellow *(Oxalis oregana)*	yellow
___ Wood Sorrel, Trillium-leaved *(Oxalis trilliifolia)*	pink
___ Wood Violet, Johnny-Jump-Up *(Viola glabella)*	yellow
___ Yarrow *(Achillea millefolium)*	white/yellow

Trees

___ Alder, Red *(Alnus rubra)*
___ Ash, Oregon *(Fraxinus latifolia)*
___ Cascara *(Rhamnus purchiana)*
___ Cherry, Bitter, Wild *(Prunus emarginata)*
___ Cottonwood, Black *(Populus trichocarpa)*

Trees continued

____ Dogwood, Pacific *(Cornus nuttallii)*
____ Douglas-fir *(Pseudotsuga menziesii)*
____ Fir, Grand *(Abies grandis)*
____ Hawthorne, Black *(Crataegus Louglasii)*
____ Hazel, Western *(Corylus cornuta)*
____ Hemlock, Western *(Tsuga heterophylla)*
____ Holly *(Ilex aquifolium)*
____ Madrona *(Arbutus menziesii)*
____ Maple, Bigleaf *(Acer macrophyllum)*
____ Maple, Vine *(Acer circinatum)*
____ Redcedar, Western *(Thuja plicata)*
____ Willow *(Salix species)*
____ Yew, Pacific *(Taxus brevifolia)*

Vines

____ Clematis, Western *(Clematis ligusticifolia)*	white
____ Honeysuckle, Orange *(Lonicera ciliosa)*	orange
____ Ivy, English *(Hedera helix)*	cream
____ Morning Glory *(Convolvulus arvensis)*	white
____ Nightshade, Bittersweet *(Solanum dulcamara)*	purple

Shrubs

____ Blackberry, Evergreen *(Rubus laciniatus)*	white
____ Blackberry, Himalaya *(Rubus discolor)*	white
____ Blackberry, Native *(Rubus ursinus)*	white
____ Blackcap *(Rubus leucodermis)*	white
____ Currant, Red *(Ribes sanguineum)*	red
____ Dogwood, Creek *(Occidentalis)*	green/white
____ Elderberry, Blue *(Sambucus cerulea)*	white
____ Elderberry, Red, fruited *(Sambucus racemosa)*	white
____ Holly *(Ilex aquifolium)*	evergreen
____ Hardhack, Spirea *(Spirea douglasii)*	pink
____ Huckleberry, Red *(Vaccinium parvifolium)*	white
____ Indian Plum *(Oemleria cerasiformis)*	white
____ June Berry, Service Berry *(Amelancier alnifolia)*	white
____ Laurel, English *(Prunus laurocerasus)*	white

Shrubs continued

___ Mock Orange, Cyringa *(Philadelphis lewisii)*   white
___ Ninebark *(Physocarpus capitatus)*   white
___ Ocean Spray *(Holodiscus discolor)*   white
___ Oregon Grape, Low *(Berberis nervosa)*   yellow
___ Oregon Grape, Tall *(Berberis aquifolium)*   yellow
___ Rose, Nootka *(Rosa nutkana)*   rose
___ Rose, Swamp/Clust. Wild *(Rosa pisocarpa)*   rose
___ Rose, Sweetbriar *(Rosa eglanteria)*   rose
___ Rose, Wood *(Rosa gymnocarpa))*   rose
___ Salal *(Gaultheria shallon)*   white
___ Salmonberry *(Rubus spectabilis)*   pink
___ Scotch Broom *(Cytisus scoparius))*   yellow
___ Service Berry, June Berry *(Amelanchier alnifolia)*   white
___ Thimbleberry *(Rubus parviflorus)*   white
___ Western Wahoo, Burning Bush *(Euonymus occidentalis)*   gr./purple

Grasses

___ Bentgrass, Colonial *(Agrostis tenius)*
___ Bentgrass, Creeping *(Agrostis stolonifera)*
___ Bluegrass, Kentucky *(Poa pratensis)*
___ Bluegrass, Rough Stalk *(Poa trivialis)*
___ Fescue, Rattail *(Vulpia myuros)*
___ Fescue, Tall *(Festuca arundinacea)*
___ Meadow Foxtail *(Alopecurus aequalis)*
___ Orchardgrass *(Dactylis glomerata)*
___ Perennial Rye *(Lolium perenne)*
___ Reed Canarygrass *(Phalaris arundinacea)*
___ Sweet Vernal *(Anthoxanthum odoratum)*
___ Timothy *(Phleum pratense)*
___ Velvetgrass *(Holcus lanatus)*

Ferns

___ Bracken *(Pteridium aquilinum)*
___ Deer Fern *(Blechnum spicant)*
___ Lady Fern *(Athyrium filix-femina)*
___ Licorice Fern *(Polypodium glycyrrhiza)*

Ferns continued

___ Maidenhair Fern *(Adiantum pedatum)*
___ Sword Fern *(Polystichum munitum)*
___ Wood Fern, Spreading *(Dryopteris austriaca)*

MAMMALS OF TRYON CREEK STATE PARK

Opossum

___ Opossum *(Didelphis marsupialis)*

Shrews

___ Dusky Shrew *(Sorex obscuvus)*
___ Marsh Shrew *(Sorex bendirei)*
___ Trowbridge Shrew *(Sorex trowbridgei)*
___ Wandering Shrew *(Sorex vagrans)*

Moles

___ American Shrew-Mole *(Neurotrichus gibbsi)*
___ Coast Mole *(Scapanus townsendi)*
___ Townsend Mole *(Scapanus townsendi)*

Bats

___ Big Brown Bat *(Eptesicus fuscus)*
___ California Bat *(Myotis californicus)*
___ Hoary Bat *(Lasiurus cinereus)*
___ Little Brown Bat *(Myotis lucifugus)*
___ Long-eared Bat *(Myotis evotis)*
___ Long-legged Bat *(Myotis volans)*
___ Silver-haired Bat *(Lasionycteris noctivagans)*
___ Western Big-eared Bat *(Plecotus townsendi)*
___ Yuma Bat *(Myotis yumanensis)*

Rabbits

___ Brush Rabbit *(Sylvilagus bachmani)*

Mammals continued

Squirrels

___ Douglas Squirrel, Chickaree *(Tamiasciurus douglasi)*
___ Fox Squirrel *(Sciurus niger)*
___ Northern Flying Squirrel *(Glaucomys sabrinus)*
___ Townsend Chipmunk *(Eutamias townsendi)*

Beaver

___ North American Beaver *(Castor canadensis)*

Mice, Rats, Voles

___ Bushy-tailed Woodrat *(Neotoma cinerea)*
___ California Red-backed Vole *(Clethrionomys occidentalis)*
___ Deer Mouse *(Peromyscus maniculatus)*
___ Dusky-footed Woodrat *(Neotoma fuscipes)*
___ House Mouse *(Mus musculus)*
___ Oregon Vole *(Microtus oregoni)*
___ Red Tree Vole *(Arboimus longicaudus)*
___ Townsend Vole *(Microtus townsendi)*
___ White-footed Vole *(Arborimus albipes)*

Jumping Mice

___ Pacific Jumping Mouse *(Zapur trinotatus)*

Dogs

___ Coyote *(Canis latrans)*
___ Gray Fox *(Urocyon cinereoargenteus)*
___ Red Fox *(Vulpes fulva)*

Raccoons

___ Raccoon *(Procyon lotor)*

Mammals continued

Skunks and Weasels

___ Spotted Skunk *(Spilogale putorius)*
___ Striped Skunk *(Mephitis mephitis)*
___ Long-tailed Weasel *(Mustela frenata)*
___ Short-tailed Weasel *(Mustela erminea)*
___ Mink *(Mustela vison)*

Deer

___ Black-tailed Deer *(Odocoileus hemionus)*

BIRDS OF TRYON CREEK STATE PARK

Ducks

___ Mallard *(Anas platyrhynchos)*

Herons

___ Great Blue Heron *(Ardea herodias)*

Doves, Pigeons

___ Mourning Dove *(Zenaida macroura)*
___ Band-tailed Pigeon *(Columba fasciata)*
___ Domestic Pigeon, Rock Dove *(Columba livia)*

Grouse, Pheasant, Quail

___ Ruffled Grouse *(Bonasa umbellus)*
___ Ring-necked Pheasant *(Phasianus colchicus)*
___ California Quail *(Callipepla californica)*

Falcons, Hawks, Vultures

___ American Kestrel *(Falco sparverius)*
___ Cooper's Hawk *(Accipiter cooperii)*

138

Birds continued

___ Red-tailed Hawk *(Buteo jamaicensis)*
___ Sharp-shinned Hawk *(Accipiter striatus)*
___ Turkey Vulture *(Cathartes aura)*

Owls

___ Great Horned Owl *(Bubo virginianus)*
___ Northern Pygmy Owl *(Glaucidium gnoma)*
___ Western Screech Owl *(Otus kennicottii)*

Swallows, Swifts

___ Barn Swallow *(Hirundo rustica)*
___ Violet-green Swallow *(Tachycineta thalassina)*
___ Vaux's Swift *(Chaetura vauxi)*

Kingfishers

___ Belted Kingfisher *(Ceryle alcyon)*

Blackbirds, Starlings

___ Brewer's Blackbird *(Ceryle alcyon)*
___ Brown-headed Cowbird *(Molothrus ater)*
___ European Starling *(Sturnus vulgaris)*

Crows, Jays

___ Common Crow *(Corvus brachyrhynchos)*
___ Scrub Jay *(Aphelocoma coerulescens)*
___ Steller's Jay *(Cyanocitta stelleri)*

Waxwings

___ Cedar Waxwing *(Bombycilla cedrorum)*

Birds continued

Hummingbirds

___ Anna's Hummingbird *(Calypte anna)*
___ Rufous Hummingbird *(Selasphorus rufus)*

Woodpeckers

___ Downy Woodpecker *(Picoides pubescens)*
___ Hairy Woodpecker *(Picoides villosus)*
___ Northern Flicker *(Colaptes auratus)*
___ Pileated Woodpecker *(Dryocopus pileatus)*
___ Red-breasted Sapsucker *(Sphyrapicus ruber)*

Nuthatches

___ Red-breasted Nuthatch *(Sitta canadensis)*
___ White-breasted Nuthatch *(Sitta carolinensis)*

Creepers

___ Brown Creeper *(Certhia americana)*

Wrens

___ Bewick's Wren *(Thryomanes bewickii)*
___ House Wren *(Troglodytes aedon)*
___ Winter Wren *(Troglodytes troglodytes)*

Chickadees

___ Black-capped Chickadee *(Parus atricapillus)*
___ Chestnut-backed Chickadee *(Parus rufescens)*

Bushtits

___ Common Bushtit *(Psaltriparus minimus)*

140

Birds continued

Kinglets

___ Golden-crowned Kinglet *(Regulus satrapa)*
___ Ruby-crowned Kinglet *(Regulus calendula)*

Vireos and Warblers

___ Hutton's Vireo *(Vireo huttoni)*
___ Red-eyed Vireo *(Vireo olivaceus)*
___ Solitary Vireo *(Vireo solitarius)*
___ Warbling Vireo *(Vireo gilvus)*
___ Black-throated Gray Warbler *(Dendroica nigrescens)*
___ Orange-crowned Warbler *(Vermivora celata)*
___ Townsend's Warbler *(Dendroica townsendi)*
___ Wilson's Warbler *(Wilsonia pusilla)*
___ Yellow Warbler *(Dendroica petechia)*
___ Yellow-rumped Warbler *(Dendroica coronata)*

Flycatchers

___ Olive-sided Flycatcher *(Contopus borealis)*
___ Western Flycatcher *(Empidonax difficilis)*
___ Western Wood-Pewee *(Contopus sordidulus)*

Thrushes

___ American Robin *(Turdus migratorius)*
___ Hermit Thrush *(Catharus guttatus)*
___ Swainson's Thrush *(Catharus ustulatus)*
___ Varied Thrush *(Ixoreus naevius)*

Finches, Grosbeaks, Tanagers

___ American Goldfinch *(Carduelis tristis)*
___ House Finch *(Carpodacus mexicanus)*
___ Purple Finch *(Carpodacus purpureus)*
___ Black-headed Grosbeak *(Pheucticus melanocephalus)*
___ Evening Grosbeak *(Coccothraustes vespertinus)*

Birds continued

___ Pine Siskin *(Carduelis pinus)*
___ Western Tanager *(Piranga ludoviciana)*

Juncos, Sparrows, Towhees

___ Dark-eyed Junco, Oregon Junco *(Junco hyemalis)*
___ Chipping Sparrow *(Spizella passerina)*
___ Fox Sparrow *(Passerella iliaca)*
___ Golden Crowned Sparrow *(Zonotrichia atricapilla)*
___ Song Sparrow *(Melospiza melodia)*
___ White-crowned Sparrow *(Zonotrichia leucophrys)*
___ Rufous-sided Towhee *(Pipilo erythrophthalmus)*
___ House Sparrow *(Passer domesticus)*

Amphibians, Reptiles, Arthropods, and Mollusks

Amphibians

Salamanders

___ Rough-skinned Newt *(Taricha granulosa)*
___ Northwestern Salamander *(Ambystoma gracile)*
___ Long-toed Salamander *(Ambystoma macrodactylum)*
___ Pacific Giant Salamander *(Dicamptodon ensatus)*
___ Ensatina *(Ensatina eschscholtzi)*

Frogs

___ Red-legged Frog *(Rana aurora)*
___ Bullfrog *(Rana catesbeiana)*
___ Pacific Tree Frog *(Hyla regilla)*

Toads

___ Western Toad *(Bufo boreas)*

Reptiles

Turtles

___ Painted Turtle *(Chrysemys picta)*

Snakes

___ Rubber Boa *(Charina bottae)*
___ Ringneck Snake *(Diadophis punctatus)*
___ Northwestern Garter Snake *(Thamnophis ordinoides)*
___ Common Garter Snake *(Thamnophis sirtalis)*

Arthropods

___ Bees, wasps

___ Butterflies, moths

___ Mosquitoes

___ Dragonflies and Damselflies

___ Beetles

___ Spittlebugs

___ Carpenter Ants

___ Waterstriders

___ Spiders

___ Centipedes and Millipedes

___ Pillbugs and Sowbugs

___ Crayfish

Mollusks

Slugs and Snails

___ Banana Slug *(Ariolimax columbianus)*
___ European Brown Slug *(Arion ater)*
___ Land Snail

If plants or animals are observed that are not contained in the checklists, please report findings at the Tryon Creek State Park Nature Center.

GLOSSARY

Accreted: To grow together, to adhere.

Antiscorbutic: A drug or agent that prevents or cures scurvy.

Awn: A stiff, bristle-like structure found on the tips of the spikelets of many grasses.

Basalt: Most common volcanic and abundant rock in Oregon. A dark-colored, fine-grained, smooth textured volcanic rock. Weathered or altered basalt may be greenish black or rusty shades of brown. Many specimens are full of gas bubbles.

Calyx: The outer leaves that surround the unopened bud of a flower.

Clone: A single individual propagated by cuttings or division (not seeds) to maintain its distinctive characteristics.

Convection: Movement of portions of a fluid as a result of density difference produced by heating.

Corduroy road: Small logs laid across a track for hauling large logs from the forest. Often called a 'skid road'.

Corolla: All the petals of a flower, collectively.

Cultivar: A clone of a species or hybrid which is perpetuated by cultivation.

Diuretic: Causing an increase in the flow of urine.

Diurnal: Active during daylight hours.

144

Drupe: A fruit like the plum or cherry with a fleshy outer part and a strong inner part enclosing the seed.

Exfoliating: Bark which flakes off or falls away, or peels off in layers.

Expectorant: Medicine that promotes the discharge of phlegm.

Faulting: A fracture in the earth's crust, the opposite sides of which have shifted past each other.

Fold: A bend, or flexure, in a rock.

Fossil: Naturally preserved remains or evidence of past life, such as bones, shells, casts, impressions, and trails.

Inflorescence: The way in which the flowers of a plant are arranged on the stem or axis and in relation to each other.

Keeled: Possessing a central dorsal ridge, like the keel of a boat.

Ligule: A projection from the summit of the sheath in grasses.

Lithosphere: The relatively rigid outer zone of the earth which includes the continental crust, the oceanic crust, and part of the mantle.

Lobe: A shallow division of a leaf or other organ.

Mantle: Layer of earth between the crust and the core.

Marsupial: Mammal that carries its young in a pouch.

Mycelial: Of or having to do with the mycelium.

Mycelium: Main part of a fungus, consisting of one or more interwoven fibers, often not visible on the surface.

Mid-rib: Main vein of a leaf.

Miocene Epoch: The geologic period that lasted from about 25 to about 11 million years ago.

Nocturnal: Active at night.

Niche: An organism's particular role within its habitat.

Ovate: Broadest near the base, narrowing rather abruptly to the apex; egg-shaped.

Ovoid: Solid ovate or solid oval; hen's egg-shape.

Palmate: Spreading like the fingers from the palm.

Panicle: A branched raceme.

Paperchases: An equestrian game or event in which riders follow a trail made in advance by a horseman scattering small pieces of paper.

Pedicels: Start of a single flower.

Petiole: The stalk of a leaf.

Petrified wood: Silicified wood; wood replaced by silica in such a manner that the original form and structure of the wood is preserved.

Pinnate: Arranged along the sides of an axis like the parts of a feather.

Plate tectonics: The theory that the earth's surface is divided into a few large plates and are slowly moving relative to one another.

Raceme: A flower cluster in which the flowers are borne along a stem or individual stalks about equal in length, the lateral flowers blossoming before the terminal bud.

Rhizome: An underground or under water perennial stem which is generally prostrate, and sends new shoots above ground each year and roots below.

Rufous: Reddish or reddish-brown.

Samara: A winged fruit which does not split at maturity. A maple capsule bearing seed.

Scarp: A cliff produced by faulting or erosion.

Serrated: Toothed along the margin with sharp forward-pointing teeth.

Sorus: A cluster of sporangia, as in ferns. Plural sori.

sp.: An abbreviaton for species.

Species: An interbreeding population of living things, each resembling other members of the population.

Sporangium: A case or sac in which asexual spores are borne. Plural sporangia.

spp.: An abreviation for more than one species.

Stolen: A runner or any basal branch that is inclined to root.

Umbel: An indeterminate flat-topped inflorescence whose pedicels all appear to arise from a common point.

Whorl: A ring of three or more similar structures radiating from a node or common point.

SELECTED REFERENCES

Allen, John Eliot. *The Magnificent Gateway - A Layman's Guide to the Geology of the Columbia River Gorge.* Timber Press, Forest Grove, Oregon, 1984.

Allen, John Eliot, Marjorie Burns, and Sam C. Sargent. *Cataclysms on the Columbia.* Timber Press, Forest Grove, Oregon, 1986.

Allison, I. S. *Late Pleistocene Sediments and Floods in the Willamette Valley.* Oregon Department of Geology and Mineral Industries. Ore. Bin V. 40 No. 11 and 12, 1978.

Arno, Stephen F. *The Mountaineers.* Seattle, Washington, 1977.

Audubon Society. *The Audubon Society Field Guide to North American Wildflowers, Western Region.* Alfred A. Knopf, Inc., New York, 1979.

Audubon Society. John Farrand, Jr., Creator. *An Audubon Handbook of Western Birds.* McGraw-Hill Book Company, New York, 1988.

Baldwin, Ewart. *Drainage Changes of the Willamette River at Oregon City and Oswego, Oregon.* Northwest Science V. 31, V. 3, 1957.

Behler, John L. and King, F. Wayne. *The Audubon Society Field Guide to North American Reptiles and Amphibians.* A National Audubon Society Field Guide. Alfred A. Knopf, Inc., New York, 1979.

Borror, Donald J. and Richard E. White. *A Field Guide to the Insects of North America and Mexico.* Peterson Field Guide. Houghton Mifflin Company, Boston, 1970.

149

Bretz. J. H. *The Lake Missoula Floods and the Chanelled Scabland.* Journal Geology, V. 77, 1969.

Burt, William Henry and Richard Philip Grassenheider. *A Field Guide to the Mammals.* Houghton Mifflin Company. Boston, 1964.

City of Portland Environmental Commission. *Our Green Home - The Resources of Portland, Oregon, 1992.* Portland, Oregon, 1992.

Clark, Lewis J. *Wild Flowers of the Pacific Northwest.* Gray's Publishing, Ltd., British Columbia, Canada, 1974.

Forbes, Richard. *An Annotated Provisional Checklist of the Amphibians and Reptiles of the Portland Metropolitan Area.* Portland State University, Portland, Oregon, 1983.

Friends of Tryon Creek State Park. *Guide to an Urban Wilderness.* Meridian Printing Company, Lake Oswego, Oregon, 1976.

Gilkey, Helen M. and La Rea J. Dennis. *Handbook of Northwestern Plants.* Oregon State University Bookstores, Inc., Corvallis, Oregon, 1980.

Gray, Asa. *Gray's Manual of Botany.* Centennial Book 1950, 8th edition, American Book Company, New York, 1950.

Haskin, Leslie. *Wild Flowers of the Pacific Coast.* Binford & Mort, Portland, Oregon, 1967.

Hitchcock, C. Leo and Arthur Cronquist. *Flora of the Pacific Northwest.* University of Washington Press, Seattle and London, 1973.

150

Kritzman, Ellen B. *Little Mammals of the Pacific Northwest.*
Pacific Search Press, Seattle, Washington, 1977.

Lake Oswego Planning Department. *Lake Oswego Data.* Lake
Oswego, Oregon, 1975.

Larrison, Earl J. and Amy C. Fisher. *Mammals of the Northwest.*
Seattle Audubon Society, 1976.

Lena, R.T. *The Petrology and Stratigraphy of the Portland Hills Silt.*
M.S. Thesis, Portland State University, Portland, Oregon,
1977.

Loonis, Walter E. and Carl L. Wilson. *Botany, 4th edition.*
Holt, Rinehart and Winston, New York, 1967.

Mathews, Daniel. *Cascade Olympic Natural History.* Portland,
Raven Editions, 1988.

Niehaus, Theodore F. and Charles L. Ripper. *A Field Guide
to Pacific State Wildflowers.* The Peterson Guide, Houghton
Mifflin Company, Boston, 1976.

Nehls, Harry B. *Familiar Birds.* Portland Audubon Society,
1981.

Oregon Department of Agriculture and Oregon State
University. *A Guide to Selected Weeds of Oregon.* 1985.

Oregon State Parks and Recreation Department. *Master Plan,
Tryon Creek State Park.* October, 1971.

Peterson, Roger Tory. *Field Guide to Western Birds, 2nd edition.*
Houghton Mifflin Company, Boston, 1961.

Robinson, Peggy. *Profiles of Northwest Plants.* Victoria House, Portland, 1979.

Sargent, S. C. *Tree Rafted Erratics Along the Columbia River.* Geological Society of the Oregon Country Newsletter. V. 19, No. 6.

Stauffer, James. *Late Pleistocene Flood Deposits in the Portland Area.* Geological Society of the Oregon Country Newsletter, V. 22, No. 3, 1956.

Whitson, Tom D., (ed.) *Weeds of the West.* Western Society of Weed Science. 1991.

Whittlesey, Rhoda. *Familiar Friends, Northwest Plants.* Rose Press, Portland, Oregon, 1985.

INDEX

153

157

158

NOTES